TOWARDS THE

AEGEAN SEA

A Wartime Memoir

TOWARDS THE AEGEAN SEA

A Wartime Memoir

Geoffrey Kirk

A SQUARE ONE PUBLICATION

First published in 1997 by
Square One Publications,
The Tudor House
Upton upon Severn, Worcs. WR8 0HT

British Cataloguing Data is available for this title

ISBN 1 899955 25 9

Typeset in Times Roman 11 on 12 by Avon Dataset Ltd, Bidford-on-Avon, Warwickshire, B50 4JH

Printed by Antony Rowe Ltd, Chippenham, England

Contents

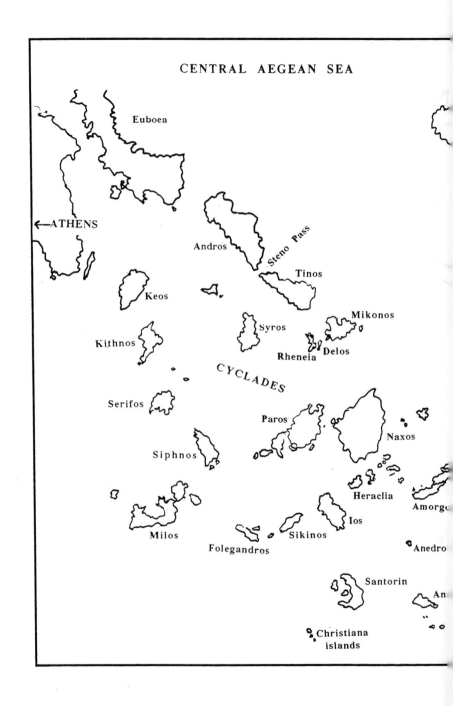

CENTRAL AEGEAN SEA

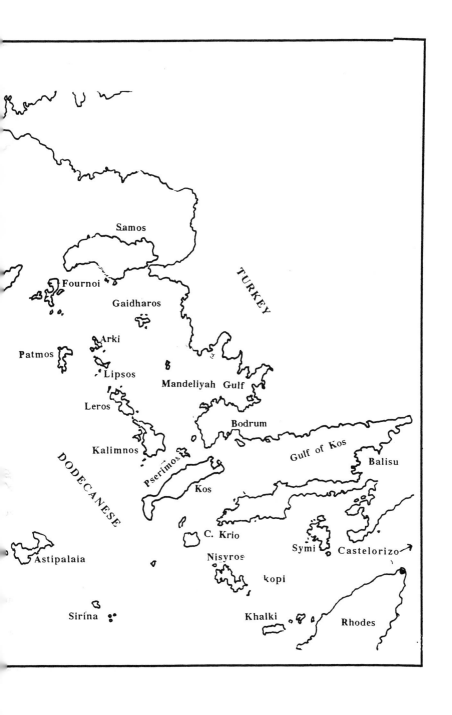

For
Robert Ballantine

CHAPTER 1

Early Days

My first attempt at autobiography was made when I was aged eight, and didn't take long. Together with a young friend called Wilson I had just written a play, and thought some account of its author's life might be in order. The play was called *Bugs and Cheese*, its hero an ancient professor who, in search of the bugs, became overwhelmed by the cheese. On second thoughts the play was abandoned, and with it, for the time being, the autobiography.

The next attempt came some twelve years later, and a few pencilled sheets of pink naval signal pad survive to prove it. Then, by contrast, the reason for undertaking such a task was not so much the perception of distinction already achieved, but on the one hand boredom (as I sat twiddling my thumbs in the underparts of the bridge of HMS Hurricane); on the other, an uneasy feeling that life, if it was to be chronicled at all, was transitory and quite possibly short. Soon this attempt, like the first, was abandoned. Now, many years later, comes a third: a partial affair, it is true, confined to schooldays and Cambridge on the one hand, the Royal Navy – still so important even fifty years later – on the other.

I was a Midlands child, born in Nottingham, self-proclaimed Queen of the Midlands, and a pair of early portraits survive from my extreme youth. They are typical of their date, the early 1920s, being carefully posed and etherially hand-coloured studio photos, in dainty gilt frames, of a little angel with the fair curls of infancy. One of these images is almost wholly beguiling; in the other the angel has a puzzled, even a slightly bloated look, and there is more than a hint of aggression. The truth may lie more in this one, for in certain respects I was (like most authors, it seems) a distinctly revolting child, once the helpless stage had been passed. The curly golden hair may have conferred an angelic appearance, but the nerve-wracking roar I was capable of emitting soon dispelled the illusion. Then I tended to throw things – books, mugs, rice-pudding – at anyone I did not like; and I was, then as now, distinctly reserved towards strangers. The sea, paradoxically in the light of later events, was another pet hatred. One of my more vivid infantile memories is of a contest with my dad when he stranded me on the seaward side of a pool on a Lincolnshire beach, in order to overcome this prejudice. In the end, of course, I won by sheer lung-power allied with tenacity of purpose.

Soon we moved to Radlett in suburban Hertfordshire, when my father, a dashing and affectionate figure called Ferdie, became chief administrative officer of the Northampton Polytechnic in London, now the City University. His family, incidentally, about which relatively little was known to my sister and myself, came not from Scotland but from north Yorkshire; while my mother's were Pentecosts, remotely Cornish perhaps but long established in Nottingham and in the dyeing and bleaching trade or allied textile pursuits.

In Radlett, at any rate, with its fashionable life centred on the tennis club (both my parents were unusually good players), one rapidly became *déraciné*. Our first dwelling there was a dreary semi-detached house on the straight, steep and prosaically named Station Road. I was still being difficult in certain respects, disliking meat and contriving to thrust lumps of it from my plate into a rather nasty dark-oak cupboard that stood behind my place at table. Eventually a strong scent of decay revealed my secret. Home-life, in most ways unexciting, was dominated by a succession of maids. Even with almost no money people tended to have a maid, even so late as the early Thirties. They did not seem to last long. One of them was found to be the secret strangler of my sister Mavis's and my pet rabbits, and had to be removed in a strait-jacket. Another, Ellen, was very nice and taught me songs from the radio, mostly from Henry Hall and his band. 'Lady of Spain, I adore you' was a particular favourite, though it seems nowadays to be rather lacking in subtlety.

Soon we moved to a much nicer house, 'Idle Dell', even nearer the station but hidden among trees and on the edge of the aforesaid dell, a deep and romantic declivity that was not idle at all, since, when I was not at school, I spent much time and energy hacking my way through its undergrowth on dramatic imaginary journeys. Later I bombarded bored crows in their lofty nests with pellets from my air-gun. Once, sheer attrition caused an elderly crow to fall out of a nest and die at my feet, at which I was horrified. Perhaps, then, I was not so aggressive after all – or education, at least, which had now begun, had tamed or removed this undesirable characteristic.

By this time school had begun to be as important as home. Generally speaking I was lucky in my schooldays – more so, it seems, than many eminent contemporaries. But that did not prevent me from being self-conscious and withdrawn at times, and in my early teens, at least, fairly unhappy. The development of a truly extroverted personality was something that took time to accomplish, and has never, to my regret and my friends' surprise, been entirely perfected.

My first school, a kindergarten, was Radlett House, presided over by the ample and kindly Miss Sharp. The keenest and most lasting impression is of wonderful Latin lessons given by her, outside in the garden under a huge lime-tree. That cannot in the nature of the English climate have happened all that often, but I do know that the declension of *mensa* 'a table' was definitely consummated *al fresco*, and an exciting lesson it was. *amo, amas, amat*, on the other hand (with its less important parts in the plural number) was an indoor conjugation; though it aroused no more interest at the time than *puer sagittam tenet*, a useful phrase which I remember particularly well. As for *puellae*, like most little

3

boys I had no special liking for them at that age. The Radlett Brownie troop looked unattractive both individually and *en masse* to this particular Wolf Cub, who was marshalled (in a dreary wooden hut on the St Albans road, with the matching Brownie hut next door), as so often seemed the case in those far-off days, by a benevolent pair of maiden ladies who cooed 'Dib dib' at one on the slightest provocation.

On the whole I got on well at Miss Sharp's school, though I remember being sent out of class into the long entrance corridor, lined with shoe-cupboards, at least twice for minor acts of disobedience. My most memorable act of defiance did not even have that relatively mild consequence. One of the teachers was Mr Geldart, who sported a wispy fair moustache and whom my mother described to me, imprudently, as 'a soppy young man'. Under some minor provocation I quoted this judgement to him, assigning its source. His riposte was swift and at the time quite devastating: 'I don't give a damn *what* your mother thinks!' It is clear to me now that this reply was both fully justified and finely attuned to the situation, though the addition of a kick up the pants might have been in order. At the time it struck me as both monstrous and unfair – not that I mean to impugn my mother's judgement, which may well, in its place, have been sound enough. As for me, in some ways I was a stupid and unsociable little boy; when we passed Miss Sharp or one of the other teachers on family walks I had a peculiar way of averting my eyes, and tugging downwards and sideways on the peak of my green school cap, that enraged my father and provoked my sister's justified contempt.

At the age of nine, with some financial help from my grandfather, I moved on to an up-market preparatory school called Shirley House, on the borders of Bushey (then quite nice) and Watford. It was a big, rambling, Tudor-style house, with some new buildings, in a huge garden with playing-fields and an outdoor swimming-pool. The owner and headmaster was Mr Campbell, a delightful and benevolent figure, Scottish but not too much so and with white hair and glasses. He was always extremely kind to me – to the other boys also, no doubt. It is in the nature of things that not all his staff were equally so, though it was an excellent school of its type and the teachers were probably above average.

Those teachers made a great impression on me (as, earlier and in different ways, had Miss Sharp and Mr Geldart). Mr Johnstone taught geography (I think) and was a large, bumbling, loose-jointed but athletic young man, no great brain perhaps but a good disciplinarian, which with small boys may be little less important. His face was bronzed, pendulous, of bloodhound cast: not unkind. The school weapon was appropriately Scottish, the tawse, and he unleashed it on me all unsuspecting one day after telling me to hold out my hand, palm upwards. I was expecting a mild ruler-slap, but this black horror must have lain in con-cealment, rolled up within the voluminous right sleeve of his baggy sports-jacket – I can still exactly visualize the pattern, a large and rather loud green check – and came curling down onto my wrist where it left four long red weals. Well, I expect I deserved it in a way, and had (I think) been taunting him a little.

Mr Pullin was smaller, neater and rather Italianate, with a handsomely aquiline nose. He too was terribly athletic and gave dazzling displays in the gym, especially on the high and parallel bars, to admiring parents who for a brief moment thought that their little Jimmy could do much the same. On those occasions he wore a tightly fitting white singlet, which revealed his pulsating biceps and magnificent pectoral muscles, together with impeccable white flannel trousers. Unlike Mr Johnstone he was a tremendous show-off, hardly academic but quite a good teacher, of English (I think) and art. Eventually he left in order to better himself by designing, strangely enough, toffee-papers. Then there was Miss Sharples the French mistress, kindly but firm with a round red face and fuzzy white hair, who had one of those outsize pencils, nearly half an inch thick, with which she rapped the back of one's knuckles if one got a bit of grammar wrong.

Yes, we were fairly well grounded in French grammar, and I still recall with gratitude some quite abstruse bits that she taught me.

The most important to me of my Shirley House teachers was Mr Hartley, a slight, dark, bespectacled and rather lugubrious man who taught me Latin. Now he *was* a scholar (later to be headmaster of King William's College in the Isle of Man), who brought my work and that of a few other brightish boys on tremendously fast, coaching me for a scholarship at Rossall – as it turned out to be. He, too, must have been at school there, since he always irritatingly referred to it as 'Ross'. He lived with his mother in Sparkford near Yeovil and came to stay the odd night with my parents, in order to keep an eye on my holiday work, when we had moved up from Radlett to Bramcote, near Nottingham again.

Games were important at Shirley House, as at most British prep schools in those days, and I have vivid memories of cricket, rugby and boxing. Swimming, too: the pool was a pleasant one, tree-lined and with a tall diving board, and I achieved a certain competence at lifesaving, or at least several certificates attesting to my skill –which I was unable to try out, years later, on the one occasion when it mattered. Cricket was run by Mr Johnstone again, no mean hand; he was desperately keen, and we played other similar schools, Elstree House and Colet Court and Orley Farm among others. Many of the eighty or so boys at my school must have had grave physical defects, for I found myself as last choice for the school XI during my final year. Yet I, too, had a grave defect (apart from being not much good at cricket), for on many summer days I was blinded by hay fever and could hardly see a thing. But I survived (with compensations – wonderful teas during school matches) until the really key match of the season came along. We had an unbeaten record; this other school, our greatest rival, was approaching our total with the last boy in. Suddenly a ball was hit firmly in my direction as I fielded at long-off. Out of the blue, disaster struck. I was seeing well that afternoon, and it had nothing to do with hay fever; simply a curious lack of control over shoulder-joint and general balance which has occasionally made itself known in later life. For I stopped the ball well enough, and then with tremendous force and enthusiasm hurled it towards – as I thought – the wicket-keeper. But somehow I swung my whole body round too far and failed to let go at the right moment, so that the ball hurtled off in diametrically the wrong direction, over the boundary in fact. This gave the match to the other side and destroyed our unbeaten record. Nothing can blot out from memory the perturbed horror revealed even by my friends, for days afterwards, and the manifest and almost manic hatred bestowed on me by poor Mr Johnstone. It was a hatred he only succeeded in getting under some kind of superficial control, greatly to his credit, many weeks later.

'Rugger' ('rugger-bugger' as my HMS Hurricane friend Billy Hutchinson was to call it in his occasional unadmiring references to the game) came under Mr Pullin's aegis, and he too ran a tight ship. Any sign of fear in approaching a tackle was ruthlessly exposed and punished. In extreme cases this took the form of requiring the offending party (or perhaps the whole scrum), after the game, to fall forward, without bending knees or putting out hands to break the fall, onto the splintered wooden floor (from which nail-heads protruded at intervals) of the boys' changing-room. He always preceded this by performing the same action himself, to show that what he was requiring of us was neither cruel nor unfair. He obviously enjoyed it, like all other forms of exhibitionism, sticking out his considerable chest so far that no harm came to him. The rest of us, though smaller, were weedier, frightened and not so canny, so that the experience scoured our knees and our chins as well as our souls. But at least I learned from all this *not* to funk a tackle – or at least not to appear to do so – and that stood me in good stead later. Pullinisms apart, I enjoyed rugby football and, as a relatively sturdy front-row forward, was not bad at it.

Finally there was boxing. I only mention it because of the extreme terror that facing up to Simmons induced in me one year. He was a nice kind boy but hugely overgrown, a full six feet at age thirteen. He had regularly caused me (and no doubt most of the others, though we preferred not to talk about it) a great deal of fright, amounting in my case, at least on my semi-blinded afternoons, to sheer terror, as a fast bowler on the cricket-field. Surely that was enough; but now I found myself drawn against him in the school boxing-contest, and my heart almost failed me. For days beforehand I sought him out and tried to engage him in sweet talk, but when the bell rang he smote me good and hard and I was quickly reduced to a battered and ignominious wreck. It was Mr Campbell himself, I feel sure, who intervened to prevent further suffering and spare the feelings of those few parents unwise enough to attend this untypically brutal and bloody function.

Shirley House was a boarding as well as a day school, so I stayed on there when I was eleven and my parents moved back to the Midlands. My father had been persuaded by my uncle Eric, by then a minor textile tycoon, to become manager of his factory (the firm was called Whiteley Stevens) at Stapleford between Nottingham and Derby. That was a wrong decision, even a disastrous one, when seen in retrospect, but it meant considerably more money than his job at the Northampton Polytechnic in Clerkenwell, so at least there was no great problem in my becoming a boarder for a final two years. I could scarcely be said to miss the boring 5-mile bus journeys from Radlett to Bushey and back each day, of which the high point was the stop near Aldenham which had a beautifully-painted poem suspended on a wooden board from a sort of gallows:

> 'As a favour, we would ask it,
> put your litter in the basket.'

It was close to there, I recall, that I later embraced an early girlfriend (Joan, was it, or Prudence?) with innocent fervour and enjoyment; but time passes, and this useful monument to tidiness and rustic Eros has been ruthlessly swept away now that urbanism has spread its ghastly tentacles into the Hertfordshire green belt itself.

Boarding, after the initial slight shock, made quite a pleasant change. It gave me more close friends than I had at home, and there were no horrible scenes or experiences in the comfortable dormitories among my largely quite civilized young school-mates. At this time I became keen on photography: nothing elaborate in the way of equipment, a simple little Zeiss Ikon folding camera – successor to an adored Box Brownie, bought in that chemist's shop, always a place of glamour for me, in the Oakway in Radlett. But when I won a relatively prestigious scholarship to Rossall (partly thanks to Mr Hartley's coaching), Mr Campbell expressed his pleasure with a splendid gift, a photographic enlarger that gave me many hours of solitary enjoyment and led to the creation of far too many wan enlargements of photos of my family, my friends, and scenes of relatively low-key natural beauty. It may have been a presage of my impending failure in chemistry that my 'fixing' solution must have been regularly too weak, since most of those images, after ten years or so, turned an interesting sepia and then faded completely. I'm sorry, because I should like to have remembered better what my school-friends looked like, and indeed who some of they were, since many memories of those years seem to have been blotted out by the more traumatic experiences of life at my next school. One boy I do remember was Ivan Hargrave; he had an exotic father, John, who published a thick novel entirely devoid of punctuation and entitled, rather fetchingly, *Summertime Ends*. John Hargrave was a keen supporter of Major Douglas and the Social Credit Party of Canada; also, apparently, of Sir Oswald Mosley, and from time to time he took a Green Line bus from his rather dank little house at Abbot's Langley to swap punches with Commie thugs in the East End. His son Ivan had a collection of little green shirts – were there a few black ones too? – that were distributed *gratis* to his puzzled friends at school. All of which shows that little boys do not understand much about politics.

My parents saved up for the occasional skiing holiday on their own, and in 1934 they met at Lenzerheide a housemaster from Rossall called J. H. Johnson. Somehow he persuaded them that, if I were to go to a public school at all, I should try for Rossall rather than Shrewsbury, which had been a previous favourite. His main reason was that on the bracing shores of the Lancashire coast I should be free from the hay fever that was still making my life a misery for three months each summer. So I eventually sat for a scholarship at that remote place, some eight miles north of Blackpool, and won £100 a year (out of the total fees, in 1935, of £145). Perhaps I should have done better to try for Shrewsbury, or indeed, as I mentioned already, stay at home and gone to St Albans School as a day-boy. In the latter case I would have had friends to play with in the holidays, and become accustomed to girls much sooner, which would have saved me a good deal of frustration and perhaps helped me to understand them better. But I received good teaching at Rossall, and its hearty traditions and stark surroundings may have been beneficial for a time … even though the hay-fever, despite the winds from the Irish Sea that flattened all vegetation for miles around, paradoxically became worse than ever.

Rossall School, founded by an Italian adventurer, was built in typically Victorian style from 1844 on, with a large red-brick Gothic quadrangle containing most of the boys' boarding-houses as well as the main assembly-hall, conventionally (and irritatingly) named 'Big School'. In the middle of the quadrangle was the rather charming stone-built Sumner library, originally the chapel; but it was too small to contain all the boys as the school, and its religious fervour, grew, and a vast new quasi-Gothic edifice was built to house our pubescent devotions in the wastelands to the south. Life in those surroundings was rather charmless, I must confess. The playing fields were extensive but bleak, the swimming-pool a huge and frigid concrete tank just inside the sea-wall, the dormitories tall, draughty and bare, with splintered wooden floors in which Mr Pullin himself would have rejoiced and over which football games of stern brutality were played on festive evenings. At least by the time I arrived one traditional Rossallian amusement, which took the form of taking it in turns to kick the shins of one's opponent until one or the other collapsed, had been abandoned as needlessly wasteful.

Another tradition, on the other hand, could in certain circumstances (if one was feeling especially well, for example) be rather fun. 'Rossall Hockey' was played on the beach at low tide, after elaborate drawings-out of the pitch in the wet sand, with crude sticks and very little passing of the puck – the players rushed round in a scrum and practically beat each other to death when they went down into the sand. But the place was not entirely devoid of comforts: we had our own studies, shared with one other boy after our first year. My study-mate for most of my time there was the tolerant and delightful J. S. Fforde, later a distinguished economist and banker. There we worked and relaxed, with many social visits between studies; on Sunday nights one made one's own supper or 'brew', creating exciting concoctions in a communal kitchen.

My housemaster Mr Johnson was a fussy man, I think it would be fair to say, but a just one. He beat me only once (for some form of arrogant insubordination again; I was astonished at how much it hurt), and made me a monitor quite early, which made life more comfortable. One of our privileges was being able to escape some at least of the dreaded 'house runs' arranged on the frequent occasions when the playing-fields were too sodden and the tide was wrong for beach hockey – horrible galumphing jogs down the muddy tracks and between the stunted undergrowth of the Fylde flatlands. I suppose we had quite fun in our monitors' common-room; it had its own fire-place, the scanty supply of coal for which had to be supplemented by nocturnal raids on the school coal-dump. This developed a taste among us for more sophisticated, but ultimately harmless, pranks and expeditions outside the school grounds in the hours after midnight.

11

Headmasters of Rossall in my day did not seem to be able to resist taking Orders (thereby saving the school chaplain much trouble; he was a splendidly gruff old bird called Bob Nevitt who found obvious difficulty with sermons). The Reverend Michael Clarke underwent manifest religious torment before his flock in chapel and made some strange decisions in his time, including the official institution of a peculiarly useless kind of note-pad to be named thenceforward, by headmasterly fiat, the Clarke Block. Carl Young, his successor, also took Orders, but was a warm-hearted man who had the gift of simplicity, talked much good sense from the pulpit, and entertained the senior boys to lavish and prolonged teas, prepared by his delightful Irish wife Norah, while we listened to the progress of test matches over the radio. He was an outstanding headmaster, and had the brilliant idea of instituting for the whole school (in two of the three terms of the year, at least) a major excursion at half-term up to the Lake District, whose southern hills could be seen in the far distance to the north on a clear day. We could choose, according to age and ability, between four or five different parties, varying from rambles over the lower fells to walks over Striding Edge on Helvellyn to hard scrambles up the rockier crests and simple roped climbs up Pillar Rock or even, on one occasion, the Needle on Great Gable. Two or three of the masters, Martin Nettleton among them, were experienced climbers, and everything in these complicated expeditions – which often involved overnight stays in places like the famous Mrs Honey's at Seatoller in Borrowdale – seemed to pass off without a hitch, which must have entailed brilliant acts of planning. I gained from those trips, as I am sure many others did, a lasting love of the Lake District and of mountain walking in general, and few other schools could have provided that.

As for more formal aspects of education, after a disastrous initial year during which I learned to abandon once and for all my own crazy insistence on trying to become a scientist (the result, I think, of beguiling but misleading 'chemistry sets' given years before for Christmas), I had good teaching there.

12

But that first year left its scars. Physics was taught, after a fashion, by a very silly bewhiskered old Scot who answered my occasional requests for guidance with the pregnant and ill-tempered words 'Ye're a scholar; ye ought to know'; chemistry by an amiable but inarticulate old codger called Mr Griffin. Somehow I passed School Certificate in these subjects, but a mildly mechanical bent was henceforth directed elsewhere as I concentrated on learning Greek and improving my Latin, at which, under the early influence of those lime-tree lessons at Radlett House and Mr Hartley later, I remained pretty adept.

That meant that I moved eventually into the classical 6th-form class of H. W. White, an eccentric figure, donnish rather than schoolmasterly, and, when he bothered to be, an outstanding teacher. He had taken a First in Greats at Corpus, knew Latin and Greek in depth (not, as I came to discover later, at all an easy accomplishment), and held forth on Thucydides, Sophocles and Horace with equal gusto and in a way that appealed to most of us. In appearance he was short, compact and stout, a rather bald Dickensian figure with a great domed forehead. When favoured pupils went to tea with him in his little red-brick bachelor house he told us gradually about a marvellous female person ('I call her "Xi",' he revealed in his curiously pedantic voice, nasal and breathy at the same time, and with a sweet smile) who lived in the Lake District and whom one day he hoped to make his own. At last this happened, when they were both I suppose in their mid-fifties, and they were married and idyllically happy thereafter. His teaching became rather more absent-minded from then on; even before that he had shown extraordinary indifference, at times, to his pupils' progress. I suppose he liked me well enough and I was relatively speaking one of his star turns, but it was not until nearly three months after I had sat for a Cambridge entrance scholarship that he stopped one day behind my desk and intoned the following question: 'By the by, Kirk, didn't you try for Cambridge before Christmas? *Do* tell me what happened!'

13

I suppose the primary impression I retain of those Lancashire years – after the first one, when I was heavily introverted and rather unhappy – is of a certain bleakness and frustration. But there were good things too, apart from the walking and climbing trips and the friendships and sometimes the classroom work itself. One was the annual visit to hear the *Messiah* in the Tower Ballroom at Blackpool. It was a great folk-ritual there, none of this namby-pamby original-version stuff, but good breezy north-British choral singing fit to bust (and some of the male singers' starched shirts did literally that in the Hallelujah Chorus). The soloists were real pros, and I particularly enjoyed the bass aria '**Why** do the Nayshuns so *few*ryusly ray-ay-ge too-oogether; and **why** do the *pipples* imahgine *yah* vain thing?'

Some of the other masters, too, lent interest to life. John Cook was an irreverent and amusing Ulsterman who lodged in Johnson's House; we did him the honour of filching his whisky on rare occasions, but he never held it against us; he was a pupil and devotee of the estimable Dr Cuttle at Downing College, Cambridge, of whom it was said that in the college's darkest days he had been Senior Tutor, Dean of Chapel, Head Porter and Butler all at once. Then there were the usual sardonic ones, like Mr Gibson who taught French, a right bastard. The music master, a man of saintly appearance known as 'Tommy', filled an almost traditional public-school role in checking from time to time on the genital development of his more favoured piano pupils (his technique being widely reported to the rest of us and causing much amusement as well as pitying contempt). Colonel Trist and Major Esnouf were splendidly military and lovable in very different ways; the latter, who ran the Officers' Training Corps, a small man who elevated himself on a white horse for special occasions. The Reverend Ted Peel, who taught me elementary Greek as well as a bit of singing, was so handsome, clever and friendly that I could never quite fathom why he found himself a school-master, and, if so, why at Rossall.

My housemaster, Mr Johnson himself, played a not

14

inconsiderable part in my education, not so much through his English classes, which were bedevilled by the need to get through set-books (fortunately 'As You Like It' was not totally destroyed for me), as because he took me and two or three other boys off to the Scottish highlands, and one year to the Pyrenees, for walking holidays, where he was a pleasant and sensible companion. Later he married the school matron, Norah Marriot, a delightful person, and after retirement at 60 moved down to Cheltenham and taught at one of the schools there – which he found almost but not quite too late that he greatly preferred to the rigours of Rossall. One of my closest friends there was the talented Michael Pocock, a good athlete and classical scholar whom I greatly admired; after the Army he went into Shell and became head of it, though it eventually killed him with a premature heart-attack.

There are things about Rossall I have almost deliberately forgotten; for example, in those days one was *ill* so much, especially in winter. My friend Fforde nearly died one January, and in a lesser way I seemed to spend weeks in bed, with measles, with mumps, with scarlet fever. At least that threw one on the mercy of other people in a generally harsh environment (which is one reason why I came to know and appreciate Sister Marriot) – but it also gave one more time to think. I quite liked thinking, and I really loved some of the schoolwork; that sounds horribly priggish, but Greek history and Greek and Latin poetry, as well as French literature which I also did for Higher Certificate (later to become A-levels), were beautiful and absorbing. Even Divinity had its moments. Most of us on the classical side continued to study it, mainly because H. W. White (who was entirely cynical about the whole topic) achieved an amazing number of 'distinctions' for his pupils by the startlingly crude expedient of dictating to us exactly which bits of the printed commentary on Ezekiel (or whatever) we were to underline, and whether with double or single strokes, and commit to memory accordingly. Not a very illuminating study, in the end; certainly it did no more than the infinitely boring chapel services to fill me with Christian fervour.

Mr White's interest in my scholarship attempt had been curiously delayed, but it did not affect the result: that I gained a minor scholarship at Clare College, Cambridge – a respectable institution, selected mainly, I think, for that reason. I was really quite ill at the time, having a slightly dicky heart and having been overworking, and experiencing bouts of adolescent disease, for months beforehand; otherwise I might have done better. But then again I might not. In any event the senior classical scholar at Clare that year was a brilliant boy from Fettes, Kenneth Maclaren, whom I naturally got to know well as soon as we both took up residence there and who horrified me by the revelation of serious mental problems, the result of terrible parental disputes and a violent father, that caused him later to kill himself.

Memories of that scholarship bid are still confused; I remember that when I reached Cambridge (not long before Christmas it would be) to sit the examination, held in the august surroundings of Trinity College dining hall, I felt very strange in the head and had to be dosed down by the famous Dr 'Fatty' Simpson in Bridge Street, a well-known Trinity man. But then I must have travelled down from Carlisle, because that is where the school had been evacuated to (to Naworth Castle, in fact, the seat of the Earls of Carlisle) in late 1939 – and yet surely when Mr White put his belated question about my success or otherwise, it was in his well-remembered classroom, complete with faded photos of the Parthenon and Athena Promachos, at Rossall itself, now taken over by the Milk Marketing Board or some such organization?

No, it must have been at Naworth, and the photos must have been moved there with all the other battered schoolroom paraphernalia. That was certainly a chaotic time, but the castle and its park and even its temporary wooden classrooms, chilled and depressing in winter, were glorious in summer, when on hot nights we slept out on the shallow lead-covered roofs behind the shelter of the parapets. We had an exceptional amount of freedom there, and I bicycled with friends all round the pretty border countryside.

One day the classical sixth was summoned over to tea with Professor Gilbert and Lady Mary Murray, who lived a longish cycle-ride away. It was exciting to meet this distinguished Hellenist (even though we had been taught to question his Swinburnian translations of lyric choruses in Greek tragedy), who disappointingly insisted on talking for most of the time about the United Nations. Other memorable teas were taken at the Lanercost Arms, a short downhill ride from the castle, where some of the happiest moments of my young life were spent. My last two terms at school, indeed, were passed mainly in the pursuit of pleasure; I could have left after sitting the Cambridge scholarship, but there was nothing much to do until I went up to Clare, and I preferred to stay on and enjoy the privileges of seniority. One of these was playing bridge; half a dozen of us were obsessed by it, read manuals on the subject and made strange preselective shut-out bids and the like. Such activities were viewed with benevolent detachment by Jim Fisher, a quizzical and amusing ex-Oundle boy (also, as it happens, ex-Shirley House) who was filling in time before reading medicine at Cambridge by teaching for a term or so, in a lowly capacity, at Rossall. Somehow I dropped this enthusiasm once and for all during the next year or two, after being drawn into games with hard-bitten adults (the last lot in Alexandria, where bridge was an obsession among the rich Greek community) who made the whole thing seem grim and slightly sinister.

Spending my last year at school at Naworth Castle rather than in the stark surroundings of the Lancashire coastal plain was on the whole a godsend, not only forcing me to adapt myself to unusual circumstances but also confirming the importance of decent countryside and genuine architecture. Some years later, when as a young don I was asked to address a branch meeting of the Rossallian Club, I delivered an impassioned speech urging that all resources should be devoted to selling up and re-establishing the school on a different site,

17

if possible close to the Lake District itself, where the boys' aesthetic senses would be less stunted. Needless to say this met with little enthusiasm, in fact I was obviously regarded as mildly insane. In any event that final school year in exotic surroundings helped to make the break from school to university a relatively easy one. Nothing made complete sense in those early months of the war, and of ripening adolescence, but I determined to try and make the best of Cambridge, at least for the single year that was left to me before my progress towards the Aegean made a more substantial advance.

CHAPTER 2

Cambridge

Cambridge during that first year there (the academic year of 1940–41 and the second year of wartime) had its ups and downs. That was perhaps the best that could be said for it. My rooms were cold and dreary; they were in the modern and undistinguished Memorial Court of Clare College (across the River Cam from the Old Court, the college's only period building but an extremely beautiful one), designed by Sir Giles Gilbert Scott as foreground to his brutal, Egyptianesque, red-brick University Library. Since I worked mainly in another relatively new and very ordinary modern building, the lecture-room block (which also housed the Classics Library) in Mill Lane, I could scarcely be said to be in close contact with the university's most distinguished and historic architecture. At least we ate in the early 18th-century dining-hall, a panelled but rather plain place, and for a short time I sang in the choir in the charming little college chapel. I had enjoyed exercising my voice at school, where one could exchange cynical glances with friends in the opposite bank of choir-stalls and for a year or two observe from close by, with mingled fascination and horror, the curiously agonized devotions of the Reverend H. M. Clarke, headmaster. At school one had a large captive audience; by contrast at Clare it gradually dawned on me that average congregations contained a mere seven or eight persons, many of the more obsessedly religious having been funnelled off by pallid and unattractive proselytizers into the austere depths of the Student Christian Movement or (even worse) the Cambridge Intercollegiate Christian Union. Moreover the little treble and alto choir-boys hired from town were as odious as they were unmelodious. Quite soon I gave the choir a miss.

I immediately made friends with two medical students, both from Shrewsbury School, Roger Dixey and Gordon Donaldson. They shared a nearby set of rooms (I had the privilege as an entrance scholar of having a small set to myself) and were fun, introducing me in addition to classical music beyond the *Messiah*: not surprisingly, the symphonies of Beethoven to begin with. Gordon was a keen rock-climber, and it seemed to be mainly for that reason that we wasted hours in each other's rooms in mantelpiece climbing (an occupation as physically demanding as it was mindless: the narrower the shelf, the harder the climb); fortunately college mantelpieces, as conceived at least by Scott, were substantially constructed. Later in the year we tried one or two of the easier 'Night climbs of Cambridge', classic routes up various old buildings, which naturally had to be conducted during the small hours to escape the attention of the Proctors and their Bulldogs.

Juvenile high jinks culminated in an act of vandalism of which I am still rather ashamed, the painting red and green of a huge and rather nice old bronze urn, a copy of one at Warwick Castle, that formed the considerable centrepiece of the lawn in front of the Senate House. Young men like to lark around, often very stupidly, and there did not seem to be enough available girls to distract one's attentions to more peaceful matters. I gazed longingly at one pretty girl during the Saturday-evening concerts in the Music School, but it was Gordon, less inhibited and with greater charm than I, who acquired her affections. Another object of my devotion was a beautiful Girton girl called Evelyn Mackenzie; she too was musical, indeed she conducted 'Acis and Galatea' in which I sang in the chorus, following her directions with admiring precision. I asked her to tea in my rooms; my gyp Sid, a practical and ingenious little man of distinctly effeminate manner and appearance, implored me beforehand not to look too bored. He had already noted the expression of world-weariness that concealed my nervousness and inexperience where girls were concerned. Evelyn eventually explained to me that she was engaged, and showed me her ring, which I had contrived not to notice. Even then I found difficulty in taking in the fact, but she was kindly and tolerant, her father a Thames pilot in whose house near Greenwich I had a reciprocal tea a year later, when I was in bell-bottoms.

A digression will explain how I came to be clad in that picturesque garb, which I had never in the past remotely imagined myself as wearing. Soon after war began my father got hold of an Anderson air-raid shelter, and I enthusiastically helped him dig a pit for it in our garden at Bramcote near Nottingham. It was a poor place of refuge, but somewhere for my mother to retreat to if my father was out with the Home Guard; in fact the whole family crouched in it one night as the German bombers flew over towards Coventry. The life it indirectly saved was almost certainly my own, and from death in, rather than from, the air. For as soon as I went up to Cambridge in the autumn of 1940 I applied to join the University Air Squadron, with a view to joining the RAF when my first year at university was finished. Two or three of my friends had already become RAF officers, and, since I was determined not to go into the Army (not because of my father's precedent, but because the crude parade-ground junketings in the OTC at Rossall had completely disenchanted me), that seemed the most obvious as well as the most glamorous choice. At some time during my first term, therefore, I duly went for a medical examination, slightly worried that my eyesight might not be good enough. It was not my eyes but my scrotum that caught their attention: evidently I had a small hernia, and was told to have it repaired and then show up again in three months' time.

The repair was duly effected in a delightful nursing-home run by nuns in Nottingham, but by then I had begun to notice that my RAF friends were to be seen around no more, not even on leave, and that caused me to wonder. One of them was Nick Peel, who with his sister Joy was one of my few Nottingham friends. He went into fighters and was soon killed in action. I was, as young men are, theoretically prepared to die for my country, but had no desire to precipitate the process unduly. Suddenly the idea of flying seemed to lose its appeal. Moreover visits to the Air Squadron in Cambridge had suggested that there was a particular RAF kind of bullshit that was not unlike the Army one. Memories of 'one up and two up' (those elemental platoon-formations that embodied the Army's highest tactical thinking at the time) were, as I mentioned, still vivid. It is true that I had quite enjoyed a couple of summer Corps camps at Tidworth on Salisbury Plain, but that was because Boy Scout tactical games were temporarily allowed to balance the tedium of forming fours, or (as it now was) threes.

So what of the Navy? I knew practically nothing about it (though around the age of ten I had been gripped by a consuming passion for model warships); but it suddenly seemed to have great attractions, comparatively speaking. Soon I appeared before a selection board, held in the august surroundings of the Senate House at Cambridge, that contained a bluff old sea-dog (could it have been Admiral Richmond, Christian Scientist and Master of Downing, in disguise?) who pointed out in graphic detail some of the discomforts in store. That aroused my obstinacy, and in any case there seemed no decent way to back out at this stage; so the Royal Navy it was. Thus was a second step taken, almost inadvertently, towards the ancient sea, the wine-dark Aegean that is, of my title.

The point of this digression is now clear: that it was digging the Anderson shelter that had almost certainly bust my gut and kept me out of the air, thus probably saving my life. But the incipient taste for flying had been a genuine one and did not entirely subside, at least until a few years later. Indeed on my very first leave from the Navy, which I spent partly in Cambridge, I managed to beg a ride at a near-by airfield, somewhere out in the Fens, in the cockpit of a Lancaster bomber practising overshoots – a relatively nerve-testing affair which I greatly enjoyed at the time.

Disappointing as that first Cambridge year was in some ways, it implanted in me a kind of passion for the place that is common enough among undergraduates, and Cambridge became my natural home for many years to come. Obviously it had a good deal to do with leaving my parental or literal home and the new freedom so gained; but also with the whole aspect and feeling of the buildings, the streets, the gardens and the river. Nowadays, from a purely visual point of view, I sometimes prefer the greater magnificence of Oxford; but in those days Cambridge had a kind of intimacy, unspoiled then by hordes of tourists, that Oxford could not match. Perhaps I am being unfair, since after many years of refurbishment and re-building, as well as experiments with one-way and pedestrian streets and the whole traffic system, Cambridge has become more manageable again, less of a claustrophobic nightmare, though French schoolchildren and Japanese camera-clickers still make it hell in summer along the Backs. It is a tiresome truism that part of Cambridge's charm depends on weather: people talk about the special light of East Anglia, something that never struck me forcibly when I lived much later in Woodbridge in Suffolk, but there is a brilliant and crystalline clarity about certain Cambridge days that is hard to parallel elsewhere. The closest I have seen is the piercing winter sunshine of Overy Staithe on the north Norfolk coast or, more dramatically still, the winter coastline of parts of New England, at enchanting Essex, for instance, near the mouth of the Connecticut River.

Part of the trouble with that first year, obviously enough, was that it was wartime. My college was half occupied by RAF cadets, there was an acute shortage of dons, indeed grown-ups of any kind seemed rather scarce, and the delightful tea-shops (like the Blue Barn, near the Round Church, where I heard the legendary John Cornford talk not long before his death in the Spanish Civil War), which had greatly impressed me on visits to my sister Mavis at Newnham a few years before, had disappeared or grown unacceptably squalid. But then one's expectations were in any case too high. A single year was too short a time for the acquisition of many new friends, and a great deal of energy had to be spent on rejecting hangers-on, one or two from one's old school, others proselityzers for activities as diverse – and as obstructive to serious work – as fundamentalist Christianity and rowing. In fact I did succumb to pressures to play Rugby football for the College, and remember some stern but enjoyable autumn afternoons spent being trampled on by large men from St Catharine's or St John's. I even got so far as playing in the Freshman's Trial, in which I did not do especially well. Perhaps the lust for self-destruction instilled by Mr Pullin was at last wearing thin.

I have already mentioned that one of my friends was the unfortunate Kenneth Maclaren, whose unhappy confidings of his mental state were not exactly cheering. I hope and believe that my unskilled sympathy helped him for a time. Another friend was George Coumoulos, twenty years my senior, to whose little flat off Emmanuel St. I went along once a week to learn some modern Greek – for I had already developed a passionate inclination to go to Greece, to the Aegean islands in particular, at the earliest opportunity, which the Royal Navy might, I thought, be able to provide. George was a graduate in chemistry who had been working in the Cambridge laboratories when Greece was invaded. He was now stuck there, fortunately with his delightful wife Eleni, but their two young children were stranded back in Greece (the boy, Dimitri, took a Cambridge PhD in soil science many years later). He was a small man, prematurely bald, wonderfully Levantine in appearance: clever, didactic sometimes to distraction, and charming. They were faithful and much-loved friends and I stayed with them at their little house in Philothei on the outskirts of Athens many times after the war. He died tragically, not so long ago, when a small plane in which he was travelling on some kind of mining reconnaissance trip (for he had become a mining engineer) crashed into the Amazon. There were only two lifebelts aboard, George went without, the other two occupants survived.

As for academic work, it was less enthralling than I had expected, too like what one had done at school and in some ways not so well taught. The lectures seemed relatively unexciting, though I went along conscientiously to hear the Regius Professor of Greek, D. S. Robertson (whose august Chair I was destined one day to occupy), on Greek drama, and the less immediately amiable A. F. S. Gow on Theocritus. Nick Hammond was the Clare classics don but he was away at the war, so we were sent for 'supervision' (individual tuition, that is) to R. M. Rattenbury in Trinity. He was a terribly nice man, as I discovered years later – a good scholar too, but a bit too mousey and reserved to make much appeal as a teacher in the individual sessions in which we went over a Greek or Latin composition in prose or, heaven help us, verse. What sticks in my mind most clearly is his comment when I told him, at the end of the teaching year, that I should not be around in the immediate future because I was going into the Navy. 'Good heavens!' he said; 'Well, I don't suppose I shall be seeing *you* again!' I don't think he meant it quite in the way it sounded, but it certainly subdued my ardour, for a moment or two, for serving King and Country. My friends, however, were quite amused, and considered it typical of 'the Rat'.

The Master was Henry Thirkill, a great Clare figure so it was said, who was quite kind in an avuncular sort of way and used to summon us, in reluctant teams of six or so, to breakfast in the Lodge, a particularly favoured segment of the pretty Old Court that faced westward across the River Cam. Conversation on those occasions was less inspiring than the view and tended to focus on silly bits of college gossip, on the quality (low) of food in Hall, and other such useless matters. It was not, after all, as though a magisterial edict would be sent straight down to the kitchens, after our mild complaints, for an extra course to be added at dinner. Thirks, as he was called, was a corpulent figure (food on High Table being obviously much better than our own) with a very large grey face and ill-fitting false teeth, unforgettable components of his almost continuous bonhomous smile.

He was less good as a host, in fact, than another Clare don who tended to issue invitations to tea, if one passed him in the Court, that were initially even more embarrassing; for they took the form of asking one *and a couple of friends*, the latter to be found by oneself. This was sometimes difficult, occasionally impossible, since the Reverend Charles Moule was notorious for the poor quality of the actual tea he served, the liquid I mean, which he made directly from a warm water tap that protruded, surprisingly, through the ancient panelling of his sitting-room in Old Court. Again, conversation did not exactly flow – but then he was clearly a very nice person, slight in build and unworldly in manner, later to become, as he still is (and looking hardly a day older) an eminent ecclesiastical scholar. The senior reverend person in college was very different, a gaunt figure of terrifying appearance called the Reverend William Telfer, later to be Master of Selwyn. He was my tutor for that year (meaning in Cambridge language that I had to check in with him at the beginning and end of term, also over any administrative or disciplinary problem), and was, I suppose, a very shy person. His great mouth would work alarmingly as he tried to find some kind of trivial words to say to his strange and uneducated young charges. Fortunately, as I thought, I did not have to visit him very often – although I know now that behind the alarming exterior was a sympathetic man. Undergraduates do not generally have time to notice such things, tending to respond to a more sycophantic approach.

As summer unfolded I sat for Part I of the Classical Tripos, which under wartime regulations could be dealt with in a single year rather than the regular two. I was awarded a first class, which was adequate, though without achieving distinction in the composition papers, especially verse composition – the knack of which (for it was mainly that, instilled by clever teaching; nearly all Old Etonians, for example, even unclever ones, were 'good versifiers') continued to elude me. Several years later I 'taught' Greek verse composition to P. M. Green, later a writer of historical novels (and a notoriously enthusiastic book-reviewer for the *Daily Telegraph*), and subsequently an excellent Greek historian, who for some reason was farmed out to me from Trinity. He was very good at the verse-composition game, and, although I could point out obvious mistakes, there were not many of those. One day his Greek iambics were less excellent than usual; consolingly I said 'Ah, well, one can't expect to be inspired every time' – to which Peter's reaction (he was a rather alarming young man) was one of great indignation: 'But I *never* write Greek verses unless I am *filled* with inspiration!' – after which there was not much left to say.

I remember little about going down from Cambridge that summer. It was a melancholy affair, obviously, and then there was a certain confusion engendered by the thought of going off to war, and in particular of returning to a presumably grim kind of schooling as an Ordinary Seaman or whatever. But, before I was summoned into the Royal Navy, part of the summer had still to be passed, and, to take my mind off things and earn a little money, I signed on with the legendary Gabbitas and Thring, Educational Agents. They duly provided me with two separate month-long assignments filling in at preparatory schools: my first experience of teaching, from which I should certainly have learned more than I did.

The first of these was near Banbury, and caused me considerable surprise because of the favoured leisure occupation of the five or so regular masters there. Summer 1941 was a time of acute beer shortages, and the warm evenings were spent by my teaching colleagues, whom I sometimes joined, as part of a highly-organized group of some twenty mixed enthusiasts. Four of them would be despatched by bicycle to the four points of the compass, to explore the beer situation in the hostelries in those directions; these scouts would release the carrier-pigeons they carried, who brought the good or bad tidings back to base and enabled the rest of us to dash off on our bikes for a suitably beer-sodden evening.

These men were not, perhaps, very academic, but at least they were ingenious. My second school was at Glastonbury and was even more curious: very unlike my own old school Shirley House. The headmaster there was suffering (as I soon learned) from some curious medical or psychological condition that made him unable to assert himself in any way, a condition of which both staff and boys took full advantage. Discipline was non-existent, and when in my second class there a particularly loathsome small boy flung some missile at me, I favoured him with a light and well-deserved cuff over the ear. Soon I was summoned to see the headmaster (for the boys reported any crime except their own), who explained in a totally remote manner that this was reprehensible. I replied equally remotely that I disagreed, and he then apologized and begged me to forget the whole thing. No doubt in a way he was right and I was wrong, but the encounter was, nevertheless, a bizarre one.

Later that evening his quite attractive but rather rapacious young daughter led me to the top of Glastonbury Tor by moonlight and tried to elicit from me some appropriate sign, in her own direction and in a different mode, of the unwonted violence I had displayed in class. I regret to say I failed to oblige her, not so much through lack of admiration as through my accursed shyness. Having been locked up at Rossall all those years and then spending the holidays at home where I met practically no young people, I took a good deal of time to nerve myself to plant even the chastest kiss – even though my contempt for girls in distant Wolf-Cub days had been replaced by an almost indiscriminate admiration of the sex.

Even more shameful, perhaps, was an episode that took place on my very first day at this particular Gabbitas and Thring *trouvée*. I arrived at the school during the lunch hour, after drinking, while waiting for a bus on the way to Glastonbury and through sheer juvenility, too much good Somerset rough cider (at, was it, tuppence-ha'penny a pint?).

There was no doubt that I was ever so slightly swaying as I made my self-conscious way through the lines of boys' tables to meet the headmaster and join the staff at the top table. I remember feeling nervous and ashamed about my condition, since I was (of course) a conventional and highly respectable young man. Then came heaven-sent relief, as it gradually penetrated my numbed mind, during that seemingly endless advance to meet my doom, that, if I was faintly pickled, then the whole of the rest of the staff, including Matron and my new Headmaster, were quite distinctly sozzled. I never learned why, and the whole thing, like much else in the shadow of Glastonbury, remained somewhat mysterious.

And so that summer of 1941 drifted on, the war news got no better, and I began to realize that within weeks I should be more directly involved. The events of the past year, and before that of my final year at school, were already beginning to seem unreal, so that when the buff-coloured envelope finally arrived, instructing me to report for duty forthwith at HMS Royal Arthur in Skegness (of all places), I was pleasantly relieved.

CHAPTER 3

The Navy and HMS Hurricane

At some stage in the process of recruitment I must have expressed an interest in becoming a Telegraphist rather than an Ordinary Seaman. I loved gadgets, felt myself to be a quick learner in some respects, and did not see myself primarily as a deck-scrubber (as distinct from deck-*swabber* – swabbing's all right). So it was to learn the secrets of that trade that I reported, in that September of 1941, to HMS Royal Arthur, alias Butlin's holiday camp in Skegness. The conversion from civilian clothes to bell-bottoms was quickly accomplished and not too painful. In some ways it was like going to boarding school all over again; though the King's Camp at Balmoral, for which I had been selected a couple of summers before, had prepared me to meet, without too much in the way of alarm or arrogance, other young men who had not had the ambiguous privilege of being locked into the public-school system. Anyway, life at Butlin's, in those days at least, was quite tolerable. The Navy had had the sense to keep on some of the Redcoats to make sure that we all found our way around from A to B, and to organise dances and other entertainments (ENSA!) on Saturday evenings. Even living in a flimsy wooden 'chalet' – with five others, was it? – was not too bad, for winter had not yet come; and the other would-be telegraphists were far from rough and tough.

In three weeks I learned how to transmit and receive Morse Code at moderate speeds, an accomplishment that has been of some but not great use in later life but which stood me in excellent stead from time to time through my naval existence. Semaphoring was also rather fun, and I picked it up quickly, though I can't claim that it has been of much value more recently. Perhaps if one fell halfway down a cliff (something that becomes increasingly likely as senility looms) the basic technique might still come in handy. The trouble is that it doesn't stick in one's automatic memory as well as the Morse Code; nor was I to live in a college named after its inventor, as happened later at Yale; nor, for that matter, can the maturing gent necessarily rely on the required agility in arm movements above head-level, even supposing someone is around to interpret them.

Suddenly, and to my immediate regret, it was all interrupted. Over the weeks, each of us had been interviewed in turn by our Divisional Officer, a sort of college-tutor type. When it came to me he turned out to be an old Clare man who insisted (not exclusively, I hope, for that reason) that I should become a 'Commission and Warrant' or CW candidate, naval jargon for a potential officer. That meant immediate transfer to a training establishment for Ordinary Seamen, since all officers had to have basic seamanship. I therefore migrated, by tortuous means involving the old London and North Eastern Railway, from Skegness to Otley Point, near Ipswich, leaving behind all my new friends. One of them, Bill Blythe from Lewes, I still remember with great affection, though I have never seen him since and he may not have survived the war; does not, at any rate, live in Lewes now.

At Otley was HMS Ganges, a regular naval training establishment for boy seamen, now lightly adapted to dealing with wartime recruits. It was an altogether less well-omened place than the innocent Royal Arthur (which still exists in name, though nowadays to be found in Wiltshire and as a training depot for Petty Officers). In quite recent years, when I lived up the River Deben at Woodbridge, I used to sail down into Harwich harbour from time to time and had ample opportunity to view once again, from close by on the seaward side, HMS Ganges and its enormous mast, as well as the long line of barrack-like buildings leading down to the water. A sense of dread persisted and still does, for me as I am sure for many others, even though the Navy has now at last abandoned the place.

The course at Ganges lasted about ten weeks and was at best tedious and unpleasant. Its main usefulness may have been to instil some sense of discipline into the young rowdies from the Gorbals who constituted much of the intake at that time. We were divided into classes of about fifty; four class-leaders were appointed for each class, a wholly thankless job for which as CW candidates I and Bill Macdonald, a married schoolmaster from Manchester a good deal older than myself, were inevitably chosen, to become objects of class-hatred as well as other kinds of resentment from the rest of the group. Our most conspicuous task was to supervise the distribution of food when it was brought down into the huts. This was separately collected by each class from a central galley and carried down in bulk to the long sheds, facing onto a wide, sloping, glass-covered corridor, in which we lived; there were more than a dozen of these class-sheds in all. Dishing out the food was a slow business, and during the process some experienced young scrounger often used to manage to slip back for illegitimate 'seconds', leaving a helping short at the end. That caused annoyance as well as short rations for the class-leaders, but was a source of much amusement to the rest – I suppose it *was* rather amusing, and if I had not been a class-leader I might just occasionally have felt the same.

In our own class we three other class-leaders tended to leave the diplomatic and patriarchal-seeming Macdonald to smooth things over, and he was wonderfully good at doing so. Another friend of mine, a Clare contemporary, who was class-leader in another hut, was less successful. Incurring the wrath of his young charges, he was sewn up in his hammock, which was then slung outside for the night in the covered way *pour encourager les autres*. This is what happened to the wretched Willems in Conrad's *An Outcast of the Islands*, and I suppose was a traditional form of seamen's punishment rather than an elaborate literary jest.

Apart from the business of sheer survival in the sheds and at the mess-tables, life consisted mainly of square-bashing, together with repetitive instructional classes on bends and hitches, how to release a lifeboat from its davits, and sundry other relatively primitive aspects of seamanship. There were also other traditional techniques to be acquired, cleaning out the 'Heads' for example, or sweeping a floor with the help of a piece of signal-pad, carefully licked down one edge so that it could be stuck for a moment to the floor-boards or lino and serve as a temporary bridge for the dust to be swept into the dustpan. About once a week we took to the waters of the Rivers Orwell and Stour (at whose confluence HMS Ganges lay) in whalers or cutters and were taught how to row navy fashion by our class Petty Officer, one of a gnarled, lazy, ruthless and mainly inarticulate gang (as I came to think of them, a little unfairly I expect) nearing retirement, to whom most of the teaching was committed and who left as much as they could in the way of discipline to us class-leaders, regardless of the fact that we had no proper authority for exercising it.

Our own PO had a disconcerting habit, when one of his oarsmen was making a particular mess of things, of pulling out the tiller with which he was steering (in a snake-like movement reminiscent of my prep-school master Mr Johnstone with his coiled-up tawse) and hurling it down the boat at him, often but not always with devastating accuracy. The rest of us, even if we were not ourselves catching the crab, had to be constantly on the look-out for this movement, which was especially provoked by the great crime of 'handling the fucking oar like a Sister-of-Mercy with a three-badge AB's prick' – a lively simile, without any question, a little technical perhaps, which should make me reconsider the general accusation of inarticulateness. It remains true, nevertheless, that imagination and vivid expression were almost exclusively confined, among these riper naval characters, to the sphere of keenly imagined sexual activity.

Life at Ganges was really rather grim. Generally speaking I absolutely hated it, though it was relieved by some enjoyable games of rugby football (at which I was not too bad and some New Zealanders in another class were very much better). Another and equally important distraction was provided by the friendship of a delightful and attractive Yorkshire girl called Audrey, a Wren in the Pay Office whom I had the good sense to 'chat up' (overcoming for once a shyness that still persisted) early in my stay when on some minor business there. Yet even her wonderful company and sympathetic support could not completely take my mind off a famous ordeal which came near the end of the course. 'Climbing the Mast' was a Ganges ritual the prospect of which blighted the lives of many young sailors and wartime trainees for weeks beforehand. This sailing-ship mast was (still is?) of enormous height, towering over the flat Essex landscape and fully fitted out with shrouds, platforms and the like, also an impressive but patently inadequate safety-net down below. Climbing the lower shrouds was straightforward enough – but then there was a massive overhang, and one had to hold on like grim death as one crawled out, upside down, over open space. Then up again to a still higher platform. Weaker brethren were reluctantly permitted to avoid the overhang and climb through a hole in the platform, not over its edge; but as a potential officer I was offered no such soft option. It is true that I had done a bit of elementary rock-climbing in the Lake District in those marvellous Rossall expeditions not so long before; but that did not include much in the way of overhangs, and in any case I have always had a moderate, not an especially good, head for heights. Time has blotted out the exact mixture of my emotions, but apprehension predominated and pride was almost entirely absent. Most of us suffered in one degree or another – all except for the privileged few with no tendency to vertigo, the élite of whom would stand on the 'pin-cushion' or tiny round platform at the very top (as indeed my brother-in-law Eric Dix was soon to do), waving in triumph to the rest of us feebler mortals down below.

Soon the end of the course drew near and lists were posted of where we were to go next. I was a 'Chatham rating', attached in theory to one of the three big naval depots in the south of England (the others, much preferable as I learned later, being Devonport and Portsmouth), and it was there that I headed for a week or so before being drafted to HMS Hurricane: a real ship this time, a powerful destroyer, not a barracks or a Butlins camp. For that I was genuinely grateful. Of Chatham itself I remember mercifully little: a truly dreadful place, Victorian, uncomfortable, soul-destroying and apparently almost pointless, with several hundreds of seamen perpetually in transit or waiting to be posted elsewhere. One of its most striking features was a gargantuan tunnel cut deep into the chalk cliff, where hundreds of us slung our hammocks and slept (I must admit) quite comfortably, undisturbed by air-raid sirens. In the morning we turned out on parade and were assigned tasks, marching around or scrubbing something, to keep us occupied for the day. There was a choice cadre of ratings who had managed to drop out of the daily roll-calls by one device or another, and lived mainly in the tunnel, lost to the Navy and indeed the world, for months and even it was said years on end. Once I caught a brief glimpse of two of them, pallid and ghost-like figures, free in their own way from the more obvious hazards of war and regarded as heroic symbols of rebellion by most of the other ratings passing through.

Soon I took train to Liverpool, a claustrophobic and fetid journey, partly by night and with long stops and inexplicable changes. Occasionally nocturnal matrons with tea-trolleys would revive one for another hour or two. Eventually our small group arrived at Gladstone Dock, where HMS Hurricane was secured alongside. At first sight she seemed enormous. Under construction for Brazil at the beginning of the war, she was taken over and finished for the Royal Navy. It was always said that much of the overcrowding below decks was the consequence of this change of use, and the extra electronic gear that had to be crammed on board; but I suspect most destroyers were the same, some (even apart from the lease-lend ones) worse. She had been damaged in an air-raid on Liverpool before ever she saw action, then had to be repaired and extensively re-fitted. Now, just before Christmas 1941, she was re-commissioned and I was part of the brand-new crew of nearly 300. That in itself was not the best of news; crews worked well when they knew each other properly and there was some sense of tradition. Certainly the crew of Hurricane never settled down, in my time at least, into a happy or a particularly efficient one.

It was terribly exciting to be on board a real ship at last. Yet living in a small mess, of about fifteen sailors headed by a Leading Seaman, occupying a tiny area, punctuated by stanchions, of one of the mess-decks, in our case just above sea-level, was a weird and claustrophobic experience. There we ate at table, sat around when off watch, and slung our hammocks at night. By archaic tradition each mess selected and paid for its rations separately, preparing the dishes (often for dinner a kind of stew, on high days or when not at sea with a rather delicious kind of dumpling called 'boily-bakes', followed by roly-poly or spotted dog), and taking them separately to the galley for cooking. That consumed a great deal of time and effort. The regular-Navy ratings in the mess knew how to do things, the rest of us tagged along rather stupidly and were generally satisfied with the results; though I always regretted that at sea, at least, there was nothing to eat, just strong tea, for breakfast, quite the contrary of the idea of 'full English breakfast' for the British working man. One of the toughest jobs in physical terms was provisioning ship; it was when wrestling with a frozen carcase of lamb or pork that I learned for the first time how to stop pussy-footing around and give out all the strength I had. But doing that towards midday with only a cup of tea in one's stomach was something of a test.

I tentatively wielded a pipe at that stage and there was a lot of smoking off-watch. Navy tobacco was both good and absurdly cheap and, with the rum-ration, was held to keep

Jolly Jack Tar happy. The rum-issue at noon, piped over the intercom with the formal order 'Up Spirits!', was the central focus of the day: a solemn and scientific affair in which the Coxswain, a slight but authoritative figure (an admirable man, in fact), dispensed from his brass-bound keg so many tots into the jar for each mess, the fierce Navy rum diluted with two parts of water to prevent its being stored up – or at least, that was the theory. Old hands knew how to preserve it for weeks on end, even so, by adding currants or sultanas. The consequence was that birthdays on board, or days immediately before returning from an Atlantic crossing, were celebrated with exceptional brio. On a few special occasions, if the weather allowed a port-hole to be opened, the meal would end in a so-called 'Yankee dish-up', which consisted of chucking most of the dirty crockery and cutlery into the sea. At least three dinners during my stay on Hurricane ended in this deplorably consumerist manner, and at least a hundred times since have I wished after prolonged dinner-parties that I could repeat the manoeuvre at home. Great care had to be taken over spoons (I think it was), since unlike knives and forks these were not classified as 'expendable' and could not therefore be ultimately reclaimed from stores without heavy payment.

Ordinary dinners, even at sea, were merely the occasion for mildly raised spirits, followed more often than not by slightly raised tempers. I quickly found that a whole tot made my head reel, and tuned into the 'sippers' system whereby one regularly gave a portion of one's tot to a friend or protector in the mess. In my case this was Able Seaman Blizzard, a mature and admirable character of rubicund and friendly features. He was a 'three-badge AB' (the badges indicating extended periods of service) who had spurned responsibility and promotion and was the actual if not the titular power in the mess, the Leading Seaman being moody and erratic. It was Blizzard who arranged mess-duties for the week: drawing the rations, preparing the food, taking it to the galley and fetching it when cooked, washing up, cleaning the deck in the mess-area, and so on. This he usually did with exemplary fairness. Just occasionally, however, he appeared to overload me, for my own good no doubt, and then I would bring into operation a despicable technique I had obviously learned from others. Saying not a word, I would silently offer my 'sippers', on the following day, to someone else. The result was always the restitution, during the couple of days that followed, of a just equilibrium on both sides.

In spite of men like Blizzard life below decks was something of a strain. A lot of the old hands were fairly bloody and could talk of nothing but booze and buggery. There was an intermittent nostalgia for life ashore, and at least conversation in that direction made a change. At mealtimes, however, the finer details of sexual intercourse were (according to a note I made at the time) the preferred topic. There was also, on that particular ship, a constant undertow of hatred for the officers, who were invariably referred to as 'the pigs' or, more elaborately, 'them pigs down aft' (which is where the wardroom was). Hurricane was not unique in this nomenclature, but it was used there with a particularly heart-felt venom that was both sinister and dispiriting.

In harbour, I was able to see something of my friends from other messes. Macdonald, the class-leader from Ganges, had also been drafted to Hurricane and I played chess with him sometimes. Another friend was Billy Hutchison, a professional actor who was cultured and delightful, also mature enough to get on better than I could with some of our tougher colleagues. But once we were at sea there was little or no time for the niceties of friendship. Even four hours on watch followed by eight hours off, the normal harbour ration, was curiously disruptive of sleep patterns. Usually at sea it was four on, four off, of which an inordinate amount of theoretically leisure time had to be spent on the clumsy system of preparing food. Even when total leisure came it was not particularly restful in those cramped conditions, with constant talk, smoke and radio music all round, except for the nighttime watches when even old hands like Blizzard needed to snatch an hour or two of sleep. I remember feeling fairly exhausted for most of the time at sea (and our convoys took between nine and twelve days each way across the Atlantic), with the movement of the ship making the simplest things difficult and one's hammock at night swinging against its neighbouring stanchion and nudging one gently or fiercely in the ribs according to sea conditions.

Partly but not wholly for these reasons, being on watch was by far the best part of life at sea, in normal circumstances at least. Here I was lucky, because the Navigating Officer, a friendly and decent man (unlike some of his colleagues, I have to admit), picked me out to be his 'Yeoman'. That meant that I spent a lot of time, when in harbour, working on charts, incorporating the multitudinous corrections that were published every week for charts for all over the world. At sea I worked mainly as one of the plot-keepers below the bridge, or sometimes as a bridge lookout; also at other more or less mechanical pen-and-paper work in the navigator's office. Whenever he took a sun- or star-sight I had to be there to write his readings down as he read them off from the sextant. That was more arduous than it sounds, since on some of our trips across the Atlantic the wintertime cloud-cover was almost uninterrupted. At the slightest hint of a clearing, day or night, the navigator had to be called, and his Yeoman with him. This could happen twice in a night if a good sight had not been obtained before, especially after two or three days of dead-reckoning. It is all different now, of course, when even a yacht can know its exact position by Navsat through a simple turn of a knob on a relatively inexpensive set. Anyway, the navigating officer's job in those days was a demanding one, especially since Hurricane was escort-leader and the Captain felt that its navigation had to be free of reproach from others, whether escorts or ships of the convoy itself. It is a cause of great regret to me that, while I can recall his appearance with absolute clarity (slight, intelligent-looking, sandy-haired), I cannot remember for certain the Navigating Officer's name (could it have been Hasler?), while far less important ones have stuck in my memory. He was an RNR Lieutenant – that is, had been in the merchant navy before the war: a wonderful man, friendly and communicative and always ready to explain things. He had the additional merit of protecting his Yeoman, when he could, from the more down-to-earth activities to which I could also be assigned, in harbour at least; tending to insist, for instance, that I should report to his office for urgent chartwork if he saw me occupied for too long in a routine deck-scrubbing or paint-washing party.

An action-station on the bridge was a wonderful bonus, with the whole ship laid out sleek and brilliant, somehow, beneath one's eyes. (Yet I also have memories of wearing anti-flash gear, and that means that for some of my time on board I had a different action-station connected with one of the 4.7" guns). Certain moments at sea were wildly exciting, in a destroyer at high speed especially – even more so, perhaps, than in a motor-gunboat, though the feeling could be comparable. That came home to me on Hurricane's first shake-down cruise, from Liverpool up to near Iceland and back, when an enormous exhilaration took me by surprise, as the purposeful and quivering shape, as much fish as machine (well, I ask for the reader's indulgence here), cut with shining bow-wave into a brilliant blue sea.

There were not to be many days like that; in fact the weather turned bad that same night. Most of the crew had been drinking far too much beer for too many months ashore. A survey the next day revealed that no more than four per cent of all hands had remained fit for duty during the middle and morning watches, with the rest heaving their guts out all over the place. I was sent down from the bridge during the middle watch, feeling none too healthy, to take a turn on the wheel in the wheelhouse below, several good helmsmen and true having already succumbed to the violent pitching and rolling. In the circumstances the forty minutes I lasted was not too bad, before the green glow and flickering action of the gyro compass repeater forced me to report myself as capable for this particular duty no longer – after chasing the ship's head the wrong way and raising agonized protests from the First Lieutenant on the bridge above. Eventually my watch ended and I staggered below. The mess-decks were a horrible sight. I still retain a vivid image of one man leaning almost unconscious over the edge of his hammock, which happened to be slung over a companion-way, and vomiting profusely into the uncaring face of another whose hammock was slung directly beneath on the deck below.

Just as there were good and bad among one's lower-deck companions, so there were (despite the universal 'pigs' designation) among the officers, even apart from the Navigating Officer whose praises I have already sung. For reasons I have never entirely fathomed, the bad undoubtedly outnumbered the good on that particular ship. Could it have been because, as an escort-leader, she carried a higher than usual ratio of regular, Dartmouth-trained officers? The delightful nature of most regular naval officers one has met since then makes that seem improbable. All the same, our RN representatives were not, most of them, an impressive bunch. That was driven home to me the very first night I spent on board, in Liverpool, when I was posted on guard-duty outside the wardroom where a farewell party was in progress. It was a pretty hectic affair, as I could not help noticing both from the noise and when I was summoned in from time to time to run various errands. The three young Wren officers there had been filled with the requisite amount of Saccone and Speed gin and were playing at one point (before being helped off to various cabins) a game which involved trying to climb over a ventilator-shaft close to the deckhead, thereby revealing enormous areas of bare flesh. Despite the roistering reputation of sea-dogs in general I was surprised and a bit shocked, not least when the three main male tacticians turned out to be all regular Navy, including the precocious and dashing young midshipman. Good clean fun by wartime rules, perhaps, but I never did care for the naval officer's *penchant* for getting his girls drunk on duty-free gin.

The First Lieutenant, an RN two-ringer, was to his credit

not one of those present on that occasion. Not altogether bad, he was nevertheless none too bright, disguising his failings with a bullying manner that was reflected in a memorably unattractive and surly countenance. There was some consolation for the rest of us in that he himself was frequently and publicly rebuked, in uninhibited terms, by the Captain. When first we joined ship the Commanding Officer had been a very pleasant-seeming man, a true Cumbrian, called Broderick. Unfortunately he left almost at once, soon after (and for all I know as a result of) rather carelessly denting the ship's bow when docking at the end of (I think) that initial shake-down cruise, back in Gladstone Dock. He was succeeded by Commander Howard-Johnston RN, whom I came to know fairly well, within obvious limits, mainly through observation of his behaviour on the bridge. He was as good at ship-handling as he was bad at crew-handling; he was also, no doubt, in many respects a good escort-leader, and for all I know much respected by other commanding officers in the group.

The ship's bridge, when we entered or left harbour, was variously compared (as I noted at the time) to a madhouse, a menagerie and a girls' school: similes not very recherché perhaps – indeed the last one remains a trifle mysterious – but all possessing an element of truth. The Captain (who, I repeat, was very good at manoeuvring the ship in confined spaces) was liable to charge from one side to the other like a lusty young bullock, occasionally knocking an officer or rating to the deck; I personally witnessed more than one such accident. Meanwhile Bell (the First Lieutenant, fattish and with facial as well as behavioural hints of Captain Bligh) and Baird (a Lieutenant RNVR, friendly, intelligent, but always shy and often juvenile) furtively clutched voice-pipes and respectively cudgelled and cajoled the wireless department to make louder the martial music with which Commander H-J delighted to inform the world that he was in the vicinity. As the volume increased, so the gallant commander became more and more dictatorial, and so did his padded bosom seem to swell.

42

Meanwhile 'Jimmy the One' (one of the kindlier lower-deck designations of any First Lieutenant) grew sulkier and sulkier as abuse was piled on his undeniably solid skull.

The Captain's greatest performance so far as I was concerned (and he was a born exhibitionist as well as a born so-and-so) was when, some three months later, we were waiting to pick up a convoy at an assembly-point south-east of Newfoundland; close, that is, to the great cod banks. We had two or three hours in hand, there were no U-boats in the immediate vicinity, and he decided to drop a depth-charge to get fresh cod for the ship. That sort of extravagance was condoned in wartime and helped break the monotony. In those days it involved getting nearly the whole of the off-watch crew, some sixty or seventy sailors, to 'man the falls' or lower the ship's whaler by rope and sheer muscle-power. It was midday, the sea was unusually calm, and no one minded delaying their dinner in order to get fresh fish. The depth-charge duly exploded on a fairly shallow setting and literally hundreds of cod floated to the surface, where the waiting whaler rowed in and collected most of them, more than enough for the ship's refrigerators. The boat then returned to be hauled up again by the two long lines of sailors. That all took about forty minutes. The whaler was duly secured in its davits and the off-watch crew had just gone down below to continue their interrupted meal when I noticed, from the back of the bridge, the Captain staring intently through his binoculars as he surveyed in a leisurely but systematic way the surface of the sea, where a hundred or so white bodies still floated. I was standing quite close behind him (one of the seven or eight people in different capacities on the bridge), and wondered just what he was up to; for he was not usually a man of relaxed habits.

I did not have to wait long, for at the end of his second sweep he straightened up and extended his right arm, his index finger inclining downwards towards one particular spot on the surface of the ocean. 'Number One,' he proclaimed, 'I will have *that* fish for my lunch!'

There was a stunned silence until the First Lieutenant,

showing a little more spirit than usual, stammered out 'You do realize, Sir, that this will mean bringing the off-duty men up again?' – to which the answer was something like 'Do you think I'm a damn fool? Do what I say, and get on with it.' Regrettably I don't remember the exact wording of this reply, though its purport and tone (not unknown with naval commanding officers, the Captain Bligh syndrome having never been completely eradicated) were as I have described them. But the '*that* fish' utterance, whole and *verbatim*, was clearly imprinted on my memory from that moment on, and was indeed much discussed afterwards, in all its pregnant simplicity, through the lower decks and (as I gathered later) in the wardroom also.

The consequences were in one way, yet predictably, an anticlimax. Sixty men were brought up on deck again, the whaler was lowered again, it was rowed out to pick up that particular fish, and eventually hauled inboard again and re-secured. The fish was found to be no bigger or better than any of the others; slightly smaller, in fact. The off-watch party once again returned below decks, this latter part of the operation having taken another thirty-five minutes. The only difference now was that the whole crew, every man on board (for news travels fast in a ship like that), was sick at heart, and what had been no more than a widespread dislike for our leader was replaced by a profound, fervent and long-lasting contempt and hatred. It may be that after I left the ship things changed in this respect, though I should be surprised if so. The whole story sounds unbelievable, yet it happened. It was not known whether the Captain particularly enjoyed his lunch, which he took by himself, of course, in his sea-cabin; but his crew's resentment took peculiar forms from then on, and not only in a general diminution of effort over the performance of many routine tasks. Thus when he had bought crate-loads of dutiable goods in the American naval base at Argentia in Newfoundland (each of the crates being duly sewn up in canvas by the bo'sun's staff), a deputation of a dozen ratings contrived to queue up outside the customs office on the dockside back in Londonderry, immediately we docked there, to apprise HM Customs of the fact. The consequence was that customs officers flocked on board and made him pay duty on the whole lot, to the enormous pleasure of the whole of the ship's company. Petty perhaps, but satisfying.

Naturally I had relatively little opportunity for effectively demonstrating to him my own reactions to his goings-on. I also had mixed feelings about him, for despite this tyrannical side he had a few good qualities and could reveal a certain charm from time to time, even to individual sailors. Also he was good at his job, questions of leadership and morale – and on one occasion of seamanship – apart, and our lives depended on that. On the other hand he was not too scrupulous over claiming a probable U-boat sinking during my relatively short time on board. Hurricane had picked up an Asdic echo and was attacking with a full pattern of depth-charges. After the second run we suddenly saw a sizable oil slick, with one or two miscellaneous bits of gear, wooden boxes, even a U-boat sailor's cap, floating up to the surface. Enormous excitement, naturally – even without a 'kill' such attacks were always exhilarating after all the discomfort and the monotony; but soon the rumour started that this was no more than a standard package released through one of the U-boat's torpedo-tubes, intended to deter further action by persuading us that the sub had been mortally hit. Repeated attacks produced no further results, and the general opinion on board – shared not only by old hands among the crew but also (as the navigator indirectly conceded) by most of the officers – was that the enemy submarine had got away. Despite that a signal had immediately been sent by the Captain claiming a probable 'kill'; its contents were leaked from the wireless-cabin within minutes of its dispatch, to be greeted with thinly-concealed disbelief by the crew at large. That claim was never modified, and did nothing to add to the Captain's popularity on board, even if it rated a Mention in Dispatches.

As a matter of fact I did at one stage have a form of

sanctions in operation against this god-like figure; but I think it preceded both the big-fish fiasco and the dubious-sinking drama. For after a brief experience of on-board life I had equipped myself with – or my mother had sent me, rather – a shiny new red thermos-flask. Before going up on the bridge for any of the night watches, which in the North Atlantic in winter were bone-chilling ordeals, I regularly made myself a flask of steaming Bourneville cocoa. On one especially icy and wave-torn night the Captain observed me pouring myself a cup of this delicious restorative (minding my own business at the back of the bridge somewhere) and sipping it with evident relief and pleasure. He himself was clearly displeased, because his own cocoa, summoned by phone-call to his personal steward in the wardroom down aft, had only just arrived after a very long delay. Moreover much of it had been spilt *en route* when the ship gave a sudden lurch, and the rest was luke-warm and congealing (as the fatty naval cocoa easily did) by the time it reached him along the wind-swept deck. Nothing was said then, but the next time I coincided with him in the middle or morning watch he again eyed my thermos ritual with unconcealed interest. The following morning his steward sought me out on the mess-deck and said that the f...ing Captain wanted to borrow my f...ing thermos – indefinitely, it seemed. I was none too pleased, but the loan was eventually agreed. After all, I depended on this man to release me for officer training when six months were up.

Thereafter I had the privilege of seeing him drinking splendidly hot cocoa out of my thermos while I had nothing. Yet he showed a crude kind of gratitude for this, and for nearly the whole of the rest of that particular escort-run he was quite civil to me. One day, however, the mask slipped and I caught the rough edge of his tongue, unfairly as I thought. So with the experience of 'sippers' and Able Seaman Blizzard in mind I firmly sought out the Captain's steward, as soon as I was off-watch during the daytime, and demanded my thermos back. For a couple of glorious nights it was I who once again had the thermos and delicious hot cocoa up on the bridge in the coldest depths of the watch – and the Captain began to display exceptional civility to me once again. I returned the thermos to his steward with nothing more said. It was a good arrangement, but could hardly last forever. The Captain was known for his ingenuity; later, indeed, he invented a simple gadget for allowing depth-charges to sink very slowly, perhaps for a whole day, to the depth at which they were programmed to explode, thus confusing U-boat wolf-packs which trailed convoys at long distance before closing in. After our return to home base he bought a thermos of his very own, bigger and better than mine, on which no comment was ever made between us.

The winter I spent on board Hurricane, the winter of 1941–2, was a particularly atrocious one for weather in the North Atlantic. The first crossing I ever made took me by surprise; after all, I had never seen really big seas before, and our ship began to feel very small in the troughs of some of those huge waves. It had all begun idyllically enough, since our base then was at Londonderry, and the voyage of several miles down the River Foyle to the sea always a beautiful one. Then began the routine of four hours on, four off, with increasing tiredness and occasional bouts of sea-sickness. Seething grey days, with the convoy scattered all over the face of the ocean as far as one could see, were followed by icy tempestuous nights. The convoy was not attacked on that particular crossing, but by the time we reached St John, Newfoundland, I was feeling that the war had begun for me in earnest. The past ten days had been, indeed, startlingly hellish (because I was, after all, just a soft little boy still), and when my watch was given leave ashore the first thing I did was to join most of my mates in queuing up at the state liquor store in town for my ration of Scotch. I've forgotten quite where in that unglamorous place we most of us got drunk; but there was no question at the time that this was the only conceivable thing to do – in order to forget, as quickly as possible, the trip that was just over. Soon I had staggered back on board and was puking horribly into one of the none too attractive lower-deck lavatories, a process I had the sense to find sordid enough never to have repeated since, at least with comparable violence.

That was, I think, the only time we called at St John. On subsequent trips the ship docked (for the turn-around period while we waited for a new convoy to assemble) at Argentia, a newly-built American naval base on the south-eastern coast of Newfoundland. My memories of Argentia are quite different from those of St John, perhaps because none of the subsequent east-west voyages seemed quite as continuously unpleasant as that first one. There was something almost glamorous about the place; the bay itself was picturesque, as indeed were the American sailors, who were also extremely friendly. They had two big base ships there, and we were allowed to use their canteen; my main memory of it was the marvellous peach-flavoured ice-cream that I consumed in profusion. There was nothing much to do in the base itself apart from eating ice-cream, but on my second visit, since technically I had the whole day off, I crammed a few emergency rations into a haversack and set off more or less at random for a walk across country. It was a brilliant day, I walked about fifteen miles without meeting a soul, and the countryside, though flattish and without many trees, was exceptionally beautiful and almost uninhabited.

That was not the only exciting walk I had in bell-bottoms; on one of our trips back to Britain we anchored in Kinlochewe on the west coast of Scotland, then proceeded to Rosyth for minor repairs. There I had overnight leave and managed to get myself to Glencoe, where I took another long walk up one of the high valleys, spending the night in the comfortable little hotel there. Glencoe itself was remote, majestic and forbidding; it all seemed wonderfully different from life on the mess-deck. There was an amiable elderly Oxford don staying there who persuaded me to join him briefly the next morning to share in his war-work, which was collecting sphagnum moss for medical dressings. The moss grew best in gloomy gullies about 2000 feet up, and I left him to it without regret.

Soon it was time to head westward again. That next trip

brought some of the worst weather of all, which was perhaps just as well, since we were being trailed, at a distance of about thirty miles, by a large pack of U-boats. Their positions were known because their radio signals were being intercepted from Portland, and one of my jobs as navigator's Yeoman was to stick little blue pins on the chart, each one representing a U-boat. That was not exactly a cheerful occupation, and I was forbidden to reveal the details to the crew. Yet knowing where the enemy were obviously made it easier, by slight changes of course, to keep clear of them. On this particular voyage the convoy had already lost one ship, a small and battered Greek tanker, which dropped slowly astern and eventually sank in the turbulent seas. As we approached Newfoundland the waves became enormous, and the whole convoy were more or less hove-to.

Nevertheless our Captain remained full of zeal, and we steamed slowly up and down the convoy, even though the chances of torpedo attack in those conditions were absolutely nil. Each time Hurricane turned across the sea in order to reverse course it was rolled heavily onto its side. At the height of the storm, just before midday, I was on watch below the bridge, ostensibly keeping the plot. The rolls were becoming prolonged and more severe; I hung on with both arms and fixed my eyes on the stopwatch that was suspended on a lanyard from the deckhead just above me. It slowly, slowly lurched upward as we rolled. The roll went on and on and the stopwatch continued its ascent. Then came the moment, to my heart-stopping perturbation, when it lay flat against the deckhead. I was clinging on especially hard by now, at this unnatural angle, but managed somehow to hoist myself upwards to the door that gave onto the port wing of the bridge, and stick my head outside and over the edge. The sight there was rather horrible. The ship was lying right over on its starboard side against the slope of a huge wave, the top of its funnel apparently only just clear of the water. It seemed to be trapped, in a position close to that of final capsize, in a great canyon of white-sheeted breakers.

So this, I thought, is *it*. We are going to sink, and just because that idiot on the bridge has to keep turning across the sea, and turning too quickly at that. Anything seemed better than that particular seascape, so I heaved myself down inside again and glared despondently at the stopwatch. After a further sickening interval it decided to unstick itself, and juddered slowly, slowly, down again from the deckhead and into a state of more natural suspension. My pulse returned slowly to normal.

After that, even our gallant Captain learned his lesson, and though we turned across the sea twice more in the next hour the manoeuvre was executed with less *brio* and with far greater caution than before. No doubt my impressions at the time were hysterical and exaggerated; I suppose the deckhead must have had a slight thwart-ship slope on it, so that we were not in fact lying at 90 degrees from the vertical but probably at 80. But that stopwatch adhering so firmly and so sedately to the deckhead, and that glimpse of the seas outside and Hurricane's relation to them, are two more of the pictures in my mind, out of a dozen or so, that do not seem to fade even a half-century later.

It is an anticlimax to describe another occasion when we were rolling badly, except that it illustrates a little of what happened on the plot. Essentially this was a large map of the whole convoy, with our own position updated all the time by course and speed. Alterations in these would be relayed down to the plot from the open bridge above, and sometimes during darkness the officer of the watch would call down and ask for a rough bearing on one of the ships on our flank. In addition, the whole convoy would usually be zig-zagging according to a set pattern: for example, 20 minutes at 270 degrees, then 30 minutes at 240 degrees, then back to 270 for a further 20 minutes. A variety of such patterns were printed in a confidential naval manual, so that all the ships of the convoy might be instructed by radio to sail on pattern 'P', for example. The plot-keepers would do the timekeeping (which was what that ill-omened stopwatch was for), and would sing up the speaking-tube 'change course fifteen degrees to star-board', or whatever, at the appropriate intervals. Sometimes the escort vessels would be doing a special zig-zag of their own on the outer edges of the convoy, which might itself in rough seas or in the absence of known U-boats be pursuing a straight course.

On this particular day there was an infernal sea running, yet Hurricane, alone of all the escort vessels, was lurching and crashing around in a particularly sharp-angled zig-zag. This time the Captain, having ordered this jollification, had retired to his sea-cabin for a short snooze, leaving the First Lieutenant in charge of the ship. After a particularly steep roll to port I decided to straighten the zig-zag somewhat and restore sanity to the situation. Thereafter at fixed intervals I was calling for 10 degrees to starboard, and so on, rather than the 20 degrees enjoined by the book. The dangerous rolls ceased, to the evident relief of the First Lieutenant, who made no comment on my obvious adjustment of the pattern but merely slowed down the ship after a time to keep in the same relative position to the convoy as a whole. I suppose this was a surprising piece of effrontery on my part, and any sensible retired naval officer who reads this will be saying to himself, with complete justification, that I was an arrogant young fool who should have been clapped in irons. But it achieved the desired effect.

Two of our number were drowned during my months on Hurricane. The first was a particularly devastating occasion. We were ploughing into one of those huge seas, a severe gale blowing from the north-west, three days short of New-foundland. I remember that I was off-watch, down below on the sodden mess-deck, when gradually an unnatural silence descended. The First Lieutenant, a rare apparition there except on his formal 'rounds', was standing in dripping oilskins, hanging onto a stanchion and shouting something. It was not easy to hear, but the message turned out to be a simple one: 'Is anyone here a strong swimmer?' Nobody moved; not many sailors were good swimmers, in any case. I thought about my own swimming prowess – it was always something I had been quite keen on – wondered a little about the implications of 'strong', and slowly put up my hand. The sailor's rule number one, 'Never volunteer', filled my mind. The First Lieutenant looked over and saw me, lurched towards me and asked 'Are you a good swimmer?', to which I replied 'Pretty fair, Sir', or words to that effect. 'Come up on deck, then,' he said, and we staggered up together.

By now the whole ship was feverishly juddering, trying to go astern. There had been no 'man overboard' over the ship's intercom, or if so it had been inaudible, but as we emerged onto the main deck amidships I looked aft and could see someone in the sea about a hundred yards astern. The bosun and another sailor were clinging on near the torpedo tubes and called me over. 'Strip off, mate,' he said, 'and let's put this on you' – 'this' being a canvas waistcoat to the back of which was attached one end of a long coil of rope. I dropped my trousers and kicked off my shoes while the waistcoat affair was laced and strapped round me. 'Look, you're a bloody fool,' said the other sailor; 'No one is going to be able to keep afloat in that sea. You're not forced to try, you know.' My teeth chattered and I looked aft. The ship was making no stern-way into the seas; the floating figure was still almost a hundred yards off. Suddenly I got a good look at his face: it was Macdonald. My heart sank into my guts; the situation was clearly desperate. The ship's stern was out of the water half the time, propellers thrashing, heavy rolling, no closer. He was still there quite clearly, floating as it seemed almost peacefully in a cradle-like trough of the waves with dense streamers of spray all round him. It was like that for a couple of minutes. Suddenly his arms were still and he disappeared. The ship stopped flailing around, the First Lieutenant came back to the midships position where I had been told to wait. 'He's gone,' he said, 'you'd better get down below and dry off.' The waistcoat was unlaced and I put on my trousers and shoes and went below. The mess-deck was strangely silent; 'It was Mac, you know,' someone said. 'Yes, Mac, I saw him,' I replied. 'Fucking torpedo-tubes again,' someone said, 'that's where they always get you.' The tubes were amidships, there were no safety-lines rigged down that part of the deck. Mac had been sent on some errand down aft and a big sea had caught him and swept him over. Later that day another sailor asked me to come up on deck, and showed me the waistcoat attached to its long coil of rope. 'Look at that,' he said: the waxed stitching which held a loop of the rope to the canvas, and which was the sole method of connexion between the two, was, on close inspection, completely rotten. 'Wouldn't have held you in that sea for more than two seconds. It's a fucking antique.'

The other man we lost was a leading seaman, one of the most vociferous critics of the pigs down aft. Again it was daylight and blowing hard; a message came down that he was to go up on deck and secure the canvas cover of the twin Browning machine guns mounted on a platform amidships, he being in charge of the team that manned them at action stations. Once again I was down below off watch, and heard his reactions (he was not in our mess, but in one close by):

'I've seen that, there's just one corner-flap loose, it's doing no harm. If I get swep over for that, I shan't lift a fucking finger to swim, you just see!' With which he went up on deck, got swept overboard, did not lift a finger, and went under for good. People who saw it said that he was moving carelessly, courting disaster, just being bloody-minded. Conditions were not so bad as with Mac, and he might have been recovered if he had managed to keep afloat for two minutes or so.

Morale was not exactly helped by this incident. In general it was low anyway; I cannot remember whether it was before or after this that the ship tried to engage a big Fokker-Wolf Kondor reconnaissance plane that came relatively low over us not far west of Ireland. Anti-aircraft capacity was not one of a destroyer's strong points in those days. The chief high-angle armament was a 3" gun amidships, which was backed up by various machine-guns. Actually the twin Brownings came into their own on this occasion, because between them they succeeded in discharging the only missile that might conceivably (if the Focke-Wolf had been half-a-mile closer) have scored a hit. That is, one of those guns managed to fire off a single .5" bullet before it jammed; all the other machine-guns on board were jammed to start with. As for the 3" gun, it fired two rounds, but the shells were just lobbed, quite slowly, a couple of hundred feet in the air before falling back into the sea. The reason for this was simple. There were two kinds of propellant charge, one for star-shell and one for high-explosive. The crew of that particular gun had a genius for loading the wrong ones, so that star-shells were almost regularly blown to pieces by too powerful a charge, high-explosive shells pushed out harmlessly by too weak a one. As for the jamming problem, admittedly it was difficult to keep salt water out of the guns in Atlantic conditions, but other ships managed it. The guncrews were duly lambasted by the officers for days afterwards, but the fact was that they did not work well because morale on board was generally poor, and morale was poor because of disastrous leadership. Or so I thought.

Six months on board Hurricane were nearly up, and I began to feel increasing relief and cheerfulness. That was the regulation period for CW candidates to do at sea before moving on to officer training. Spring in any case was approaching, and the thought of a spell ashore followed by some completely different kind of ship was deeply attractive. One day at about this time the Captain was showing some other senior officer over the ship while we were briefly in harbour. I was fiddling around with the plot, and the Captain as he walked past stopped and said to his companion (with typical insensitivity to my feelings) 'This is one of our CW candidates; there's some nonsense about releasing them after six months, but they're very useful ratings, and I don't believe in that.' My heart sank, and as soon as I came off watch I reported this dread news to the other three CW ratings. They were equally appalled; I was not alone in finding HMS Hurricane heavy going. Billy Hutchinson looked grim and said he was going to try to do something; it transpired that he had a powerful family friend in the House of Commons. I had spent three or four days of leave with Billy and his friend Paul at their pretty house in Hasker Street, and knew that they knew lots of important people, so I didn't take this threat as mere bragging.

Some pencil-written notes on the back of a pink signal-pad recorded, in a horribly pretentious style, my feelings at the time, and also some of the peculiarly mixed ways I proposed for dealing with them. 'It is now quite certain that I shall have to undergo another trip. The prospect of another six or seven weeks of boredom and repression is appalling, but I console myself with the thought that if I ever get as far as a wardroom, and its accompanying physical, if not social, comforts, it may be in the Arctic or the Far East or god knows where . . . Although at the moment I'm angry and disappointed at the casual neglect which has produced for me another trip on this irksome vessel, I am already managing to force on myself a more 'philosophical' frame of mind. Of course this is made easier by the fact that we are now lying at anchor in the most perfect weather, just off Rothesay – the loveliest part of the lower Clyde. Things will not be so easy when we get to sea, and the programme of reading I have made out for myself [including *Northanger Abbey* and *Tristram Shandy*, it appears] will not be so easy under the régime of watch-keeping, lack of sleep, and that curious listlessness which always seems to overcome one after a few days at sea. – The company on board has lost much of the charm of novelty. The incessant talk about homosexuality, discussed in more than usually perverted detail, becomes a trial; it always crops up at meal-times, and it takes some more delicate subject to make our rather solid roasts and duffs and spuds really palatable. The officers, of course, are as peculiar as ever.'

Soon we set off for another Atlantic crossing, fearing that this would be our way of life for the indefinite future. Providentially the weather was a great deal better and life at sea easier than usual. After nearly a month we were back in

Britain, then the miracle happened. Within twenty-four hours of docking (it was at Liverpool again, for some reason) a signal was received that all CW candidates on board were to report, after a week's leave, to HMS King Alfred at Shoreham – that was the training establishment for those in line for commissions. Billy Hutchinson's appeal had worked: his eminent friend had raised questions with the Admiralty which had led to rapid and totally unexpected action. Suddenly we were ashore, hammock and kitbag and all, and life became rose-coloured once again. I was sorry to say good-bye to Able Seaman Blizzard, to my teacher and benefactor the Navigating Officer, and to many others; but the thought of an altered way of life was irresistibly attractive. Added to this was the escape from what had been a deeply uncomfortable seven months, boring and terrifying by turns. The former greatly outdid the latter, as it happened, and I was lucky in this respect. No doubt a certain amount had been learned, and I was not quite so priggish and juvenile as when I joined Hurricane. But the day I got ashore was the happiest of my life up to that point, and I do not believe it has ever been completely surpassed in anything that has happened since.

HMS Hurricane was sunk in the Atlantic on Christmas Eve, 1943.

CHAPTER 4

A Commission, and Coastal Forces

The names of naval shore establishments were often confusing, sometimes more than a little absurd. HMS King Alfred
was more so than most, representing an improbable combination of Lancing College in West Sussex followed by the
Hove swimming pool (emptied, of course, and divided into
scores of little rooms and hutments). Ludovic Kennedy claims
that it was the Hove underground car-park, an easy mistake.
Nautical excursions were undertaken in Shoreham harbour
nearby. The first part of the course at Lancing contained too
much high-class parade-ground stuff for my liking, and was
less than enthralling. What stands out most in my capricious
memory is an encounter I had with the naval chaplain there, a
solemn fellow called the Reverend D'Eath. I had started trying
to teach myself the piano, since (by one set of rules, at least)
we cadets were allowed to use at certain hours a grand piano
in the huge chapel that is that school's greatest ornament.
There I was slogging out a simplified, inaccurate but to me
rather moving version of 'Jesu, joy of man's desiring' one day
when the Reverend Death came in and commanded me
instantly to cease. I was, he said in an deeply unpleasant
manner, defiling the House of the Lord.

Admittedly the sounds I was making were not exactly
celestial, but the sounds Bach envisaged certainly were, and I
thought that good intentions might count in my favour. I could
have been right, since two days later there came an unexpected
sequel. Some tremendous religious and naval occasion

57

required us all to attend chapel. The front rows were occupied by officers and other grandees, the cadets filling most of the rest of the vast building. The Reverend Death was conducting proceedings. Everything seemed to be going well when, at a point where the Almighty was being invoked in especially urgent terms, there was sudden and unexpected silence from the direction of the altar. Everyone looked up from their prayerfully crouching position to see the reverend figure in obvious difficulties. His mouth was working alarmingly but no sound came forth. It became clear that he had been struck dumb; eventually, indeed, he had to be replaced by an acolyte. It was hard for me, although not in one of my strongest religious phases, to avoid seeing this as some kind of punishment sent from on high for his unfeeling abuse of a couple of days before. At the same time one could not help feeling sorry for the poor fellow.

At Hove the teaching became more intense, with a good deal of navigation and relatively advanced seamanship (interspersed with further details of that basic nautical manoeuvre, almost as sacrosanct as the Army's 'two up and three up', if more complicated and rarer in its satisfactory achievement, of releasing a lifeboat from its davits). Elements of what was known as officer-like behaviour began to be inculcated, along with the rudiments of discipline as it was to be exercised over Other Ranks. How to conduct a court martial was briefly but lovingly touched upon.

The time passed swiftly; evenings in Brighton were agreeable enough in those days, and for odd weekends I stayed in London with Billy Hutchinson and his delightful South African friend Paul, in 9 Hasker Street, where the rising young actor Dirk Bogarde was a lodger. Eventually we sat our final examinations; at that stage of the war young officers were much needed, and few of us failed. Then came the great day of passing-out, arrayed at last in officer's uniform and with the acting wartime rank of Sub-Lieutenant RNVSR. Finally we were despatched to the banks of the Thames for two weeks of ultimate polish, applied in the elegant surroundings of the

Naval College at Greenwich. There we dined in Thornhill's great Painted Hall and were served by WRNS waitresses and generally taught our manners at table and how to behave like little gentlemen. It was now the late summer of 1942 and I was really quite keen to go to sea again.

In the Navy a certain amount of choice was allowed, within reason and depending on availability, over what kind of craft one might serve in. I had already opted for Coastal Forces (namely motor launches, motor torpedo-boats and the like), since that gave one the greatest chance of responsibility and freedom as a junior officer – also of having as little as possible to do with Dartmouth-trained RN types after my depressing experience of them in HMS Hurricane. I hasten to repeat that this experience was no doubt to a large extent untypical, but it did, fortunately for me as I believe, colour my choice at a critical stage in my embryonic naval career. Be that as it may, Coastal Forces were officered by wartime-only characters for the most part, and I thought this would suit me very well. My first appointment was as First Lieutenant to an HDML, a so-called harbour-defence motor-launch, a useful 72-footer that was actually employed for all sorts of tasks, including, when in foreign waters (and despite their eleven-knot maximum speed), that of gunboat. I took a rapturous trip down the Thames and up the east coast in that craft, then for some reason was immediately transferred to a bigger kind of ML, the no less famous Fairmile B type, all of 112 feet long, that was just finishing building in Brightlingsea where I now joined it. These boats had two officers and about twenty crew, and my Captain was called (let us say) Lieutenant Seeker RNVR. As though to disprove my crude distinction between RN and RNVR, he was a difficult red-headed man, bombastic and boastful, not wholly incompetent but deeply unlovable, as I must have confided to a friend in the little base ashore. That had unexpected consequences three months later, my friend on the shore staff (himself no admirer of Seeker) having evidently taken matters into his own hands and filed some kind of report about temperamental incompatibility.

Before that, however, we had sailed up to Scotland and through the Caledonian Canal (a marvellous experience with its enclosing mountains and succession of lochs and locks), spending Christmas at Inverness as part of the working-up programme. I went ashore as much as possible in the evenings, to keep out of my commanding officer's way and avoid the necessity of pouring the gins-and-limes (a junior officer's privilege in the curious hierarchy of the Royal Navy) in the earlier phases of his regular seduction sequences in the wardroom he and I shared. After a week or two of rather enjoyable training on Loch Long, we moved on to the final part of the working-up programme at Tobermory in the Isle of Mull. Here, from his base in the Western Isles Hotel, reigned a famous figure, Captain 'Monkey' Stephenson, who roamed around the harbour in a dinghy in the middle of the night to test the alertness of ships' sentries. Needless to say, ours were not impeccable. His idea of gauging the cleanliness of a galley was to pull out a drawer and scrape around at the back of its recess with the end of a new matchstick, which was then withdrawn and held up for all to see as no longer quite pristine. Severe punishments were imposed for such lapses, and his charges eventually proceeded on their way with tattered nerves but defensive measures against such incursions greatly improved.

In the end our ML and its two companions arrived at beautiful Milford Haven to join the rest of the flotilla, outward-bound for Freetown in dampest West Africa. I was looking forward to the trip, if not to Africa itself. One advantage of it was that Seeker and I would be alternating the watch-keeping and therefore see relatively little of each other. Then came the change of fortune at which I have hinted. The day before we were due to sail I was summoned to see the flotilla commander, who showed me a signal instructing me to proceed at once to take up a new appointment as First Lieutenant of a motor-gunboat building at Teddington. I was delighted and surprised. Questioned about possible reasons for this late transfer, I could only suggest that it was because of my mild and unofficial grumbling, back at Brightling-sea and months before, about my commanding officer. The flotilla commander (a Lieutenant-Commander RNVR and an obviously humane man) then confided that he entirely shared my view on this subject. It was evidently his firm intention to dump the gentleman ashore at the earliest possible opportunity – but not before the continent of Africa, pre-ferably at its most remote and dismal outpost, was reached. Evidently he, like me, had suffered from my CO's panic about leaving for foreign parts. In my case the Seeker stratagems mainly took the form of obviously faked fits of acute stomach-pain and the like, which he called upon me (vainly, I'm afraid) to report to the flotilla medical officer. To be out of range of this unsavoury figure was a blessed relief, even though it meant leaving the crew and other friends in the flotilla.

The new boat, MGB 673, was nearing completion in Tuff Bros' yard at Teddington, and that meant that we, its future

The crew of MGB673.

occupants, could get the finer details of fittings in wardroom and mess-deck, as well as on the bridge, finished more or less as we wanted them. It was rather like fussing over a new yacht. These D-class boats, which were powerful and relatively stable, if not particularly beautiful, with a top speed of around 29 knots, had three officers. My new commanding officer, a very different kettle of fish from Seeker, was a friendly and impressive figure called John Barker, a thirty-year old with a lot of yachting experience behind him. The third officer was even younger than I, the amusing and cynical Guy Hamilton, who had already studied briefly under Jean Renoir and later became a well-known director of James Bond movies. He and I got on extremely well, and I still have a copy (on the ubiquitous pink naval signal-pad paper) of a poem I composed at sea in honour of his 21st birthday:

When Youth to cold Discretion's Part achieves,
Then Industrie must triumph o'er brute Sleep:
Nor shall the Chart-strewn Couch, where Morpheus weaves
Amid the dusty Tomes his Web, e'er keep,
Fond Hamilton, thy Slothful Corse. Awake!
The Day of Manhood dawns; th' uncharted Deep
Demands thy vaunted Skill. Machines forsake,
All fallible Devices of thy Trade, and weep
Thine errant Course, more Sinuous than the Snake
That caused thy double Share of Sin. Nor fail
In good Resolves this Birthday Morn – the first
And twentieth since Thou thrust, unasked, thy pale
And miserable Frame upon the World. Let *Worst*
Give way to *Best*; in moral Wise, redress
The Balance of thy Maid-despoiling Years.
('Never been done' – how false a Claim, express
The reproachful Eyes of Puss: devirgined Tears
Proclaim *undone* thy Victims, lecherous Guy!)
Be this thy Goal: a Humble Life and Chaste,
Kept straight by Lodestone's Lore and *wakeful* Eye;
And so Delights of many a Birthday taste.

I cannot now recall exactly what verse-form I was attempting to mimic, if any; the pastiche was, after all, composed rather rapidly on a windy night. But it contains exactly 21 verses, so I must have been trying hard – or simply lucky. It should be explained that a course worked out by Guy as Navigating Officer, with the help of various fallible implements like the parallel ruler and the hand-bearing compass, had needed mild adjustment. We were somewhere off the Eddystone Light at the time, and he was now snatching a well-earned rest on his bunk by the chart-table in the wheelhouse (with the 'dusty Tomes', that is, various navigational handbooks, on a shelf above him) after his labours. 'Never been done' refers to a traditional song much loved by sailors, which includes the words 'Twenty-one and never been done, queen of all the Fairies'. I had forgotten about the ship's cat, a regrettable innuendo intended to symbolize his startling success with various girls, one or two of whom I had myself vainly tried to impress.

Life in terms of accommodation was less comfortable than in a B-class ML, except that the Captain had a tiny cabin of his own; Guy and I bedded down in an excessively cramped little separate wardroom. Once again the crew, as well as we officers, had to be trained, but not with the full working-up programme in Scotland. At one point, as Gunnery Officer, I spent a few days in a factory near Swindon learning the finer points of the power-mounted twin-Browning and Oerlikon turrets, as well, supposedly, as giving a boost to the workers there. Then we spent a week secured alongside Westminster Pier so that the boat, relatively new in its class, could be demonstrated to their Lordships of the Admiralty. When two or three of these gnarled and august characters arrived, the sophisticated armament of power-driven turrets and the like did not arouse nearly so much interest as the good old-fashioned hand-operated 3-pounder gun that stood, relatively useless, an almost antediluvian affair, on the after deck. Otherwise the week afloat in central London, with frequent 'runs ashore' and a good deal of money in the pocket after the eremitic sojourn in fashionable Teddington – not to mention the spurious glamour conveyed by our shining and conspicuous craft – was quite memorable. My dinners seemed to be taken either in a good Swiss restaurant in Soho or, when I wanted to make an impression on myself or others, at Prunier's.

Quite soon this boat was in action of a kind, because we found ourselves, *en route* for somewhere as part of our working-up programme, in Great Yarmouth on the night of its heaviest air-raid. John Barker had gone ashore and left me in charge when the raid, obviously unexpected, began. All naval craft had to cast off from their berths alongside and mill around in the narrow River Yare. This was difficult in itself because there was a strong tide running and I was not too experienced at handling the boat – also it was excessively dark, except for the intermittent searchlights, and everyone else in the river seemed almost equally out of control. There was a good deal of cursing and swearing, but actual collision was somehow avoided, by us at least. The tactical scheme was that we were all meant to fire enthusiastically when the red lights along the quay went on – or off? Nobody seemed to know. Urgent instructions of 'Watch the red lights!' kept coming from the loud-hailers ashore; I think we were among those who opted to fire, in a pretty random manner (the bombers in any case being out of range), when the lights were on. The rest blazed away when the lights were off. Then in addition one of our gunners managed to get the muzzles of his twin Vickers machine-guns under, rather than over, the safety rail that was meant to prevent him from shooting up his own craft. Bits flew off the mast but no damage, fortunately, was done to personnel. Ashore, of course, things were different. Eventually the bombers went away and nerves slowly, quite slowly in my case, recovered.

MGB 673's eventual destination was Dartmouth. After a brief and rather pleasant sojourn in Brixham we were based across the river there in an uncomfortable trot on the old coaling pier at Kingswear, and for a few months did routine anti-E-boat patrols in the western part of the English Channel, while intermittently fuming at the powers that be (ultimately C-in-C Western Approaches) for not using us, rather than or together with bigger ships, in sweeps against enemy shipping round the Channel Islands. But the higher échelons of the Admiralty (I think it could be said) were slow to grasp all of the potential of Coastal Forces, and nothing happened except that these ill-conceived sweeps resulted in the loss of a light cruiser and at least one Hunt class destroyer. As for us, no doubt our routine patrols (the last of them to be described more vividly in a few pages) were useful enough in their way, especially in deterring mine-laying E-boats; but fortunately we occasionally had the additional and more obviously rewarding job of landing agents over in France.

We did this on three or four occasions, onto a beach just below the dominating and (in wartime at least) formidable-looking Cap Fréhel, a few miles west of St Malo in Britanny. The Germans had strong shore defences there, but did not seem to expect this sort of minor impertinence. Getting to and fro, past the Channel Islands, was quite a long crossing, made less interesting than it might have been because manifestly aggressive acts were actually forbidden us in much of this sector of the Channel. The idea was to make the enemy feel more peaceful there, and so facilitate covert landings. Once or twice we came across tempting targets in the shape of small German coasters, but had to leave them alone. I remember one in particular, a gleaming and obviously quite new ship, that we came upon unexpectedly some seven miles off the French coast, on a rather misty night when our radar was obviously not working too well. We passed down its starboard side, on a reverse course, at a speed of about 18 knots and a distance of about 150 yards. Our guns were quickly on target, but no one on board that ghost-like vessel seemed to notice us, or to realize what a very lucky escape they were having as we proceeded firmly but regretfully on our way.

The agents, either singly or in pairs, were brought down to Kingswear on the afternoons of departure by their escorting officer and one or two obvious plain-clothes policemen (with genuinely large boots, I noticed) from London. These would then go through a solemn final examination, at which our Commanding Officer was present, to make sure their clothes and luggage had no tell-tale labels. Usually they took bicycles with them, or at least the spare tyres that were always much needed by the Resistance. On one occasion the official minders contrived to overlook a large 'Paddington-Plymouth' label that remained fastened to one of the bicycles stowed on deck; I derived a certain mild amusement from pointing out the oversight to the Special Branch. The trips themselves could sometimes be rough, and all our agents, with one exception, were atrocious sailors. Once we had a pair, of which one belonged to the Communist, the other to the right-wing Resistance. I had strict instructions that they were not to be allowed to meet – one was stashed away in the Captain's cabin, the other in the wardroom – but after a couple of hours at sea they were both puking into the same lavatory basin. Once they had recovered a bit they seemed to become the best of friends.

The agent who was *not* sea-sick was a Frenchman with the *nom-de-guerre* of Victor, who spoke reasonable English. He was, at first sight, a disappointing figure, tiny in build, with fine yellow hair and something of the air of a bouncy Spaniel pup. He entirely lacked the reserve that I had assumed was proper to his trade, as I kept him company in the wardroom before going up on watch. Naturally I was curious to hear about what he expected to find ashore, and how he, and the friends who were meeting him, were to penetrate the coastal defence belt behind the landing beach. Such topics were forbidden, but the conducting officer who up to now had controlled his stream of conversation was out of the way, nursing his own sea-sickness in the Captain's cabin. One or two prompts from me were enough to set Victor going, and the next hour passed like a flash. At one point he slid down the fastener of his leather jacket and produced from under his left arm-pit a minute teddy-bear, the genuinely smooth and furry sort that were already difficult to buy.

'My mascot,' he announced, in a highly histrionic manner. 'I carry it wherever I go; it is for my daughtaire.'

I did not say much, my attention fixed on the machine-pistol that hung in an ancient holster under his other arm-pit. He was left-handed, then; more to the point, the gun and the bear between them must have been awfully uncomfortable. Eventually I commented that he did not look like a married man; at which it transpired that he was neither married nor engaged, but proposed to look for a fiancée near Bordeaux, in the part of the *Maquis* for which he was headed. The girls there were said to make good wives. The whole flamboyant story sounded like a film-script; certainly it was a practised affair, but it kept his morale up and I did everything a willing listener could do to help.

At the end of the hour it was my watch up on the bridge, and I saw no more of Victor till we had dropped anchor under the lee of Cap Fréhel, when he scrambled down into the bouncing rubber dory and, sitting astern of the two seaman, waved good-bye and slipped off into the darkness. I was sorry to see him go. After ninety minutes the dory returned with the news that he had not been met as arranged, but that after searching for his friends for some time he had, quite against orders, gone on his way. The conducting officer uttered some horrible oaths and had much to say about Victor's ability to get through on his own, together with the chances of his misappropriating the half-million francs in his suitcase if he did. Somehow I guessed this to be unfair, and was not sorry to see the last of the city gent when we berthed back at Dartmouth nine hours later.

A couple of months after this episode I happened to encounter, in the outer office of a branch of Naval Intelligence in London, an Army Captain who might, I thought, have news of Victor. After expressing surprise at my enquiry (since we were not supposed, in the MGB, to look upon our obscurer passengers as more than temperamental pieces of baggage) he gave me the news I had asked for, and in surprising detail. It was unpleasant news. Victor was dead. He had been killed by machine-gun fire on a wooded hill-top some fifteen kilometres east of Bordeaux, when he and another member of the *Maquis* were transmitting a radio report. The Germans were almost all round them in the darkness before they realized the danger. Both ran for what looked like a gap, and when the soldiers opened fire Victor pulled out his famous machine-pistol and fired back. It was this that probably did for him, since his companion, who had not tried to shoot, escaped.

Two other episodes under Cap Fréhel have become slightly blurred by time. In one we were waiting interminably for a small boat that should have been launched to meet us from the shore. The MGB was lying silently at anchor, with engines stopped, about half a mile offshore and a mile to the east of the cliff-top, where the outlines of fortifications could be clearly seen. There was starlight but no moon – these landing or pick-up operations were confined to moonless periods; but the waiting was tedious, and a bit of a strain. Dogs could be heard barking along the cliffs, and from time to time dim lights appeared. Guy Hamilton and I were sitting facing astern, with our backs against the after side of the bridge, drinking cocoa, leaving John Barker to scan the scene through binoculars and curse the extended wait. It was agreed that another twenty minutes was the most we could risk. Barker was getting a bit agitated, but then he had the responsibility for deciding these things and we did not. Suddenly he thought he saw something and, without waiting for confirmation, called down the engine-room speaking-tube for a crash start. Guy and I silently cursed him as we took up our action stations. Those gunboats had four 1250-horsepower Packard engines which were exceedingly noisy when they were all started together; usually they were started one by one. Anyway, we were obviously heard. Great activity became discernible from on top of the cliff as our foredeck hands hastily upped anchor: shouting, more lights, more dogs barking, eventually a couple of searchlights. By this time we were withdrawing gracefully, and returned home to Dartmouth in one piece – but unlikely to be altogether popular back at base, since the landing-beach had been partly compromised.

And yet it was on that same beach, I feel sure, that we nearly had to leave Guy Hamilton behind. He had gone ashore with the rubber boat and was delayed by some muddle with the receiving party ashore. Time was tight, but in the end he made it. On his next boat (as he wrote to me later) he was less fortunate and was abandoned to the care of the shore party, after which he was absent for several weeks. Fortunately, apart from being a resourceful young man, Guy had the advantage of a French mother and was almost bi-lingual. There had been little difficulty in finding his way, under the care of the Resistance, to Paris, where he waited for a month in a safe house till he was spirited back to England. During that interval, it transpired, he sampled the traditional pleasures of Parisian life, having, in short, a whale of a time. I thought at first that there might be an element of exaggeration there, but, apart from his command of the language, Guy was an unusually debonair figure and a great one with the girls. Most of what he wrote was probably true.

On another of these agent-landing trips we had an extra passenger aboard. He was an American observer, a naval officer of fairly senior rank, of whom I was put more or less in charge for the night. I could not help admiring his intrepidity; he did not, after all, *have* to go on this jaunt, as the rest of us did, but had come along, it seemed, more or less for fun. Actually his indifference to possible danger amounted to an almost complete unawareness of his surroundings. Soon after being shown the wardroom, and the spare bunk for when he needed it, he spotted a book of mine in the book-case: it was Hemingway's *To Have and to Have Not*. It turned out that Hemingway was a friend of his, and he decided to re-read the novel then and there. He put his feet up on the bunk and for the next three hours disturbed my own attempted slumbers at regular intervals with one unchanging remark, made in tones of unbounded good humour and admiration: 'Gee, Ernie's tough!' I had enjoyed that particular novel before (unlike some of the others), and have always especially liked it since, with those three pregnant words in mind. Eventually, the book re-read, my American friend made a brief visit up to the bridge; we were just approaching the French coast, it was excessively dark and rather cold, and he retired below again for a little sleep precisely three minutes thereafter. He did not wake till we re-entered Dartmouth the next morning, and said good-bye after a hearty breakfast with an air of obvious satisfaction at an observation mission well accomplished.

The final stage of the career of MGB 673 (in its first commission, at least) is recorded in an account I wrote for my own purposes soon after the end of the war, which at the risk of one or two repetitions is set out here more or less in full.

'In the late summer of 1943, as a young Sub-Lieutenant RNVR, I was First Lieutenant of an MGB operating in the western part of the Channel, out of Dartmouth. Quite often, a pair of our boats would be sent out on defensive patrol about fifteen or twenty miles off the coast. The main object was to deter mine-laying E-boats, which had caused trouble along the Channel convoy-routes. But our lives were complicated by the fact that from time to time our new-fangled radar stations ashore would detect unauthorized craft (or, occasionally, friendly craft mistaken for such, or even, indeed, persistent seagulls) many miles out at sea. The MGBs, which would perhaps be lying stopped if the weather was fine, or cruising slowly along a fixed patrol line, would then be "vectored" (or in plain language directed), by a simple code over short-wave radio, onto a course to intercept the intrusive echo. None of this was work any of us particularly fancied, being dull and uncomfortable; and even if we came across an E-boat, the chances were that, in fine weather at least, its speed of some 32 knots would enable it to escape our own slightly slower boats.

The Eddystone Rock (its lighthouse unused of course in

wartime) became the main focus of these dismal but no doubt necessary excursions. The Commanding Officer, John Barker, the Navigating Officer, Guy Hamilton, and myself would loll disconsolately round the bridge (or rather, we two younger ones would), feeling too cold or too hot, too hungry or too thirsty, sure that nothing would happen, occasionally listening over the intercom to the grumbling of the men on watch up and down the deck or crouched in the machine-gun turrets at each fore corner of the bridge, by the twin Oerlikon mounting amidships or in the shadow of the Bofors gun on the foredeck. We were usually allowed to set off back home around 4.30 a.m., when any enemy craft would themselves be seeking their own part of the sea. Normally the two boats on patrol would cruise slowly into the narrow mouth of the pretty Dart estuary just as the early workmen were cycling off to work. Then with a good deal of shouting the gunboats would turn round in the river and come up alongside the other boats of the flotilla beside the unfriendly piles of Kingswear railway jetty. Guns would be cleaned, hoses connected, decks washed down. A large breakfast would be eaten; one might feel virtuous but slightly fractious. In the afternoon one would sleep restlessly, in the evening, perhaps, sample the limited pleasures of pro-vincial wartime amusement – the cinema, the under-stocked pub, the occasional Wrens' party. Dartmouth and the estuary were of course delightful, but hardly lively.

That is what normally happened on defensive patrols. The night in question was different. It started off windier than usual; the weather forecast had not been a bad one, but by midnight a stiff north-easterly was blowing, a moderate sea was running and small craft were beginning to feel uncom-fortable. In really bad weather the patrols would usually be withdrawn. John Barker, senior officer of the two boats, was not a man to request permission to return to harbour before he had to; so we continued cruising up and down very slowly in line ahead, two or three miles off the Eddystone Rock. Down below crockery broke, scuttles leaked, deckheads dripped. Along the deck and through the intercom oaths of none too pretty a nature were almost drowned out by the howl and clatter of the wind and the thud of passing seas. Knees became tired through balancing against the pitch and the roll; the supply of cocoa gave out; the cook came out on deck and swore brutally. There was a strong general feeling that no sensible German would be abroad on a night like this.

What *would* be somewhere around were three Free French motor torpedo boats, of a smaller brand than our own D-class Fairmiles (which could be completed either as MGBs or as MTBs); they had been sent cross-Channel earlier in the evening but would certainly now be forced to return. It was known from their radio messages that they had become separated from each other by the bad weather; one was even now approaching Dartmouth. For another half-hour we persisted; then the MGB astern signalled a tactful enquiry about the possibility of returning home. At last John Barker decided that duty was done – but almost at the same moment a radar vectoring-message came over the short-wave radio. An echo had been picked up about twelve miles to the east of our position, and our two boats were ordered to proceed on an interception course at best speed.

A degree of restrained abuse greeted the receipt of this information on the bridge; less restraint was noticeable when it was passed by me, as First Lieutenant and Gunnery Officer, to the various action stations. A single craft heading for the coast was almost certainly the second or third of the three separated French MTBs, and it was no night to provide plotting-practice for the Wrens on radar-watch ashore. Yet the order could not be disobeyed, and at some ten knots our two craft turned into a head sea, drenching and awkward enough even at that speed. The people ashore, we persuaded ourselves, must know what they were doing; they must have special reasons for knowing that the French boats were *not* the cause of the suspect echo. So the crew were closed up again to action-stations, except for the fore-gunners who, unable to do any good on a spray-swept focs'le, clung to the rail further aft, under the lee of the bridge.

After ten minutes the weather was noticeably worse, and we stoically faced up to the prospect of a sticky hour or two. Then came another whistle from the radio-cabin speaking-tube; a fresh vectoring code-word had been received. It contained the simple order "Increase speed by ten knots." Barker growled and ordered a four-knot increase, after relaying the order by radio telephone to the boat astern. Our own boat started plunging deeper into the slanting seas, white and threatening at this speed as the waves came juddering in fine on the port bow. Steering became difficult and the Coxswain at the wheel muttered to no one in particular that he was sweating heavily under his f...ing oilskins. Thick, almost solid spray hurtled across the bridge. I stood behind the plexiglass spray-shield with my face partly muffled in a speaking-tube, ready to communicate with the guns' crews. Suddenly from the boat astern, slewing from side to side about a hundred yards back, a white light showed itself.

'Message, Sir,' I shouted somewhat fatuously at the CO.

'What the hell is he playing at, using a white light? Number One, flash him to communicate by R/T and in any case only to use a blue light.'

John Barker was obviously right; flashing a bright light in the direction of a hypothetical enemy, even if in this case a probably mythical one, was stupid. I flashed away, holding on with one arm to a projection on the bridge, the water seeping into my oilskins as I did so.

Eventually a blue light acknowledged receipt and a new signal was made: 'W/T room flooded, radio out of action.' That was too bad; the same thing seemed likely to happen to us, since bits of wave were coming over solid now, and the mess-deck forrard already had a small lake swilling around in it (as I was informed without much delay by some of its indignant occupants). The Captain decided to reduce speed by three knots or so – even that would make a considerable difference – and I was told to flash the order for a similar reduction to the other boat. Just as I was in the middle of this, an especially violent wave threw me off balance for about two seconds. I erased the word and went back to the one before. The other boat was even slower in receiving, obviously having difficulty in picking up my small hand-signalling light. Suddenly it began pulling away to port, up into the wind. At the same time it must have increased speed slightly and gradually began to draw level with us.

'Perhaps he wants to flash us with the white light again,' I shouted; John Barker merely grunted, wetly. Then through the storm we heard a dim voice – they were trying to communicate by amplifier, not by any standards a good idea in the circumstances. Naturally we could only make out an odd word or two. Their boat was clearly visible now – we could even see the mouth of the loud-hailer turned towards us. He was getting rather close, only fifty yards away, exactly abeam, our own boat now doing around thirteen knots (still too fast by normal rules of seamanship, but this was a supposed emergency); the other slightly more, since it was still carrying way from the surge of speed to draw level.

Ten seconds or so passed; then another big sea came in and hit us, but we kept our course. A moment later we saw the silhouette of the other boat shorten dramatically, its bow wave showing white and approaching fast. Obviously that same sea had momentarily slewed its bow towards us. The distance was alarmingly small. The Coxswain bore down hard on the wheel, trying to swing our own boat away to starboard. The other gunboat failed to straighten. On the bridge all of us suddenly realized it was going to collide. 'Look out,' we shouted, as much to that looming unhearing shape as to each other. I tore my headphones off and clung on tighter; their stem hit us hard, full abeam, just by where I was standing. There was an almighty crash, and the whole boat rocked right over to starboard, gunwale under, and shuddered horribly. More bizarrely still, a human figure came hurtling over from their foc'sle and landed on our deck. I recovered my senses to see the stem of the other boat within two yards of my own feet and close up against the foot of the mast, just at the back of the bridge itself. It had sliced clean through almost half the width of our hull.'

That is as far as my typed account goes. I have altered the wording a bit here and there, but have not disguised the clumsy suppression of the other boat's identity and that of its Commanding Officer. That was out of chivalry, or perhaps prudence, I suppose. Fifty years onward some Freudian protection-mechanism keeps them blanked off still, though her number must have been close to our own 673. Her Captain's Christian name, at least, I *do* remember (perhaps for his general amiability as much as for his temporary lapse): it was quite undoubtedly Nigel. Be that as it may, Nigel must have felt a bit abashed about the whole affair, which, apart from being rather terrifying at the time, was wasteful, expensive, embarrassing and potentially dangerous. That is, it left us thirty miles out in the Channel (the various vectorings having taken us far out beyond the Eddystone) with dawn not too far away, a dirty sea, and our own boat nearly bisected.

As so often, the vessel causing the collision came off relatively lightly; the bows of those light wooden craft were naturally their strongest part. Fortunately, as Nigel went hard astern and wrenched his stem out of our deck, our boat as a whole seemed to be maintaining fore-and-aft rigidity. The engine-room was flooded and we had lost all power, we were low in the water but not sinking. And miraculously no one had been hurt. Miraculously, too, a voice came out of the darkness saying that the other boat had sustained relatively much less damage and could tow us. Getting lines aboard was not easy and took half-an-hour or so, but Nigel started to display some of the seamanship that had seemed so strangely lacking in his earlier manoeuvres. Eventually we were under tow, making about three knots, with the sea, mercifully, on the quarter.

It took till late the following afternoon to regain Dartmouth. There was a certain anxiety during some of those daylight hours that a passing German plane might spot our predicament. Luckily that did not happen, and eventually, dispirited and exhausted, we managed to secure our maimed and waterlogged craft alongside the Kingswear jetty. In the course of that seemingly endless journey the names of Nigel and his ancestors had come in for a good deal of comment, from all 32 of us aboard our boat (and 30 aboard his, no doubt; we still retained one of his seamen). What was cruelly clear was that MGB 673 would have to be de-commissioned and virtually re-built. All the months spent in training an initially rather raw bunch of seamen were wasted, and my heart sank; so no doubt did those of John Barker and Guy Hamilton, of the Coxswain and Bosun and Chief Motor Mechanic and many of the rest of us on board. 'Costly Farces', as Coastal Forces operations were affectionately known among ourselves, seemed all too true, and it would be months before most of us were likely to get afloat again – if, that is, we stayed in similar craft. That prospect, because of the possible delay, did not greatly please me. The time had come, I felt, to review my options for the future.

CHAPTER 5

The Demise of MGB 673,
and New Openings

A few weeks before the partial sinking of MGB 673 I had
been present at a conversation in the officers' mess ashore
which turned to the question of naval appointments – for
officers, that is: how such appointments were made, how
erratic they were, and so on. One of those present claimed
that he had arranged his present job, which he enjoyed, almost
single-handed, by calling direct on the Admiralty in London.
It sounded unlikely, and I queried it.

'Yes, in Queen Anne's Mansions,' he repeated. 'I just went
along there and was shunted round from office to office till I
arrived at the one that did the appointments down here. I
explained what I wanted and they seemed only too glad to
help.'

Back in Dartmouth, camping out in a ruined boat and
knowing that a fresh appointment might be coming through
after a week or two of paying-off leave, I pondered the future.
Did I want to join another MGB, or perhaps an MTB this
time? I adored the boats, but felt frustrated by the turn of
events, and in particular did not fancy joining another new
craft with a long and tedious working-up process to be gone
through. Then there was another and quite different element
in the equation. The idea of Greece was often in the back of
my mind; my contact with the Classics so far, at school and at
Cambridge, had made a curiously deep impression, reinforced
with what reading of Greek I had been able to do in off-
moments on board Hurricane (for the most part). I loved the

idea of ancient Greece and had a romantic desire to have a hand in liberating its modern successor: all very Byronic, in a modified middle-class sort of way. So I decided to use the first couple of days of my leave for doing what my acquaintance claimed to have found so easy, by going up to London and trying to wangle an appointment to the eastern Med., to some kind of small craft operating close to Greece itself. For a junior officer to put himself forward in this manner might seem impertinent and even improbable; but the whole business of life in the Royal Navy was relatively new, the Navy itself had its surprisingly flexible elements (as well as some very inflexible ones), I was young and confident and willing to try anything, and in any case there was little to lose.

Queen Anne's Mansions was a vast red-brick building, and I started off at the first office on the left on the ground floor. There I explained my purpose to an extremely nice Lieutentant-Commander RN, who turned out to be in charge of pay for the WRNS. He suggested I should try five doors further down, which was at least concerned with appointments – but only, it transpired, in home waters. Nevertheless the reception there was equally friendly, and I was referred to the floor above. There I hit upon an office actually concerned with Mediterranean personnel; but when I explained that I wanted something preferably concerned with the occupied Aegean they seemed to think this to be a matter for Naval Intelligence, so I was sent round to an address in Victoria Street to consult the oracle at DDOD(I): an acronym full of alliterative mystery, which stood (I found) for Deputy Director, Operations Division (Intelligence). I refreshed myself with a light lunch before plunging, a shade more warily than before, into the gloomy office block. Almost at once I found myself talking to a mildly exotic figure, a Lieutenant RNVR who was also a baronet. He certainly had something to do with intelligence-gathering affairs in the Eastern Mediterranean, but interrupted the even flow of our pleasant conversation by suddenly asking, in languid tones, the following question:

'Kirk, if you happen to be captured, do you terribly mind being shot?'

The rather absurd form of his question was (I have afterwards thought) extremely helpful to me, since the only answer any sane man could make was 'Yes!' – and this is the one which, politely but firmly, I gave. If my interlocutor had said, for example, that of course the sort of work he had in mind for me was potentially dangerous, with possible capture to be avoided at all costs, then my public-school upbringing and recent infusion of officer-like qualities would quite possibly have led me to make subservient and ostensibly heroic noises, implying that this was just what I was looking for. In fact my nerves *were* relatively good and I should probably have meant something like that, having had no great feelings, when I entered the building, about possible extra danger involved in intelligence affairs or proximity to occupied Greece. But being a spy in the full sense, heavy disguise, firing-squad, the lot, lay beyond my immediate scheme of things. At all events the answer I gave, combined with my obvious desire to fulfil at least some of the conditions he had in mind, led the gallant baronet to refer me, quite politely, to another office on the floor above.

Now at last I felt I was getting somewhere. This office was larger than the others I had visited, having a couple of Wren secretaries (neither of them distractingly pretty), one of whom showed me after a time into an inner room where sat an amiable-looking, quite elderly Commander RN. He had already been briefed over the phone from my last port of call, and after eliciting a few more details about my career, and why exactly I was at a loose end, he breezily announced, 'Ah! This sounds like the Levant Schooner Flotilla to me.'

That seemed promising. I had never heard the name of this outfit before (the brain-child of its romantic founder Adrian Seligman), and it instantly suggested that I should need lots of sailing experience, which I did not have. But the Flotilla seemed to operate from Beirut and Turkey (the latter of course being technically neutral, but with a blind eye turned from time to time) up and across into the Aegean. That was where I wanted to be, sailing experience or not. The Commander had to leave for another appointment, so he arranged for me to return the following morning. In fact I was told to arrive an hour and a half early, to give me the opportunity of reading through some of the office files on the work and personnel of the unit in question. Compared with my previous visit to the baronet, I seemed to be making real progress. Yet what the Commander did *not* tell me, and what I remained quite vague about until years after the war ended, was that Hitler's infamous 'Commando Order' made it highly probable that one *would* at this stage of the war have been shot if captured (as Allan Tuckey was), even in uniform, in Levant Schooner Flotilla or Special Boat Squadron operations or any other kind of commando or irregular warfare. Whether the Commander's omission of such considerations in favour of more social ones was due to ignorance or cunning on his part I do not know, but in any case I was by now quite blithely committed.

Those files, when I came to read them, certainly did not reveal anything about possible treatment if captured, but were of unexpected fascination in a quite different way – not so much over what the Flotilla actually did (which remained curiously vague), but about the characters and social dispositions of its officers. Some of the information, as I found out later, was rather out-of-date, and a few of the figures mentioned had moved on elsewhere. But the tone was remarkably frank, resembling that of a private detective agency more than anything else. The sexual peccadilloes of certain of the more senior officers (none higher in rank than Lieutenant-Commander) were reported in surprising detail, and sharp judgements made on the general efficiency and operational capacity both of these and of their junior colleagues. Quite what my Commander friend here in London thought that I should learn from all this, and why it should come before the eyes of a very junior potential recruit to the Flotilla, absolutely defeated me. None the less I accepted the gift when it came, and could only suspect that the Commander himself had not examined those files recently, if ever. The curious lack of reality about everything DDOD(I) knew, or thought it (or he) knew, about the Flotilla only became evident later. Suffice it to say here that when I eventually arrived in the Middle East to join the group, everyone was amazed at who had appointed me, why they had done so, how they knew anything at all about the Flotilla, and in particular who the hell was DDOD(I)? All this confusion did not cause any resentment against me personally, because the people out there were mildly flattered to think that their unit and its activities were somehow known about in London, within the whole structure of Naval Intelligence, and that an office in this venerable institution was busy keeping some sort of record of their existence. It seemed prudent *not* to reveal that the main and most detailed interest seemed to be focused on operational activities of a purely psycho-sexual kind.

Further conversation with the Commander was evidently satisfactory, and he seemed to think there was no difficulty in removing me from Coastal Forces into the eastern Mediterranean orbit. 'But before we send you out there,' he said, 'are there any Courses you would like to do?' After a moment's thought I replied that I would like to brush up my navigation (never too good) and also, if possible, extend my rudimentary modern Greek a bit. No difficulty was envisaged, provided I could arrange the latter for myself. The consequence was that, after a week's leave with my parents, I went down to HMS Dryad at Portsmouth (the Navy's navigation school) and spent ten rather pleasant days further proving to myself that, despite all my experience of being Navigator's Yeoman on HMS Hurricane, actually taking a star or sun sight myself, and working it out correctly, was generally beyond my powers. In the final theoretical test I managed to place my ship somewhere just to the north of the Mendip Hills, close in fact to where I am living now as I write these words. Fortunately navigation in the Aegean was a question of pilotage, rather (land never being too far away), and 'making with the sextant' was rarely if ever needed. Meanwhile I had consulted the gentle and agreeable Professor John Mavrogordato at Oxford, and he had arranged for me to spend a couple of weeks there talking Greek to the brother (once consul in Smyrna, now retired) of R. M. Dawkins, his predecessor in the Chair. My friend Harold Cox, whose comfortable rooms in Lincoln College were vacant (he being away on war-work in London), allowed me to use them, and I spent a sybaritic and thoroughly profitable two weeks in Oxford. Lincoln's kitchens being closed, I ate lunch and dinner in Brasenose, where Maurice Platnauer and Stanley Cohn, both of them amusing and cynical friends of Cox, provided relatively distinguished and sometimes unusual conversation.

Despite this competition, the most intriguing social event of my stay was dining one evening with R. M Dawkins himself in Exeter College. Dawkins, who had the grand title of Bywater and Sotheby Professor Emeritus of Byzantine and Modern Greek Language and Literature, had first made his name excavating the sanctuary of Artemis Orthia in Sparta, and was extremely good company. He was also, without a doubt, more than mildly eccentric: a Cambridge man by origin, I am pleased to say. Up in his rooms after dinner he spent a good deal of time trying to persuade me to visit, on his behalf, the Crusader castle of Krak des Chevaliers, if and when I might happen to be on leave in the Lebanon, in order to copy down for him some inscriptions so obscene, according to my informant, that they had not yet been published. I promised to do my best (a promise I was never able to fulfil), and shortly afterwards, perhaps under the weight of this obligation, suffered a relatively violent nose-bleed. Dawkins was most obliging and eventually produced a long and rather dirty white rag to staunch the flow, a rag which in the end I absent-mindedly put in my pocket, throwing it away when I regained my rooms. A couple of weeks later, just before proceeding abroad, I received a typewritten post-card containing simply these words: 'I wamt my tue, RMD.' Subsequent enquiry showed that both the style and the accuracy of the great man's typing, and his addiction to not very clean white ties, were typical.

I had been instructed to return to the London office of DDOD(I) before leaving for the Mediterranean, and it was arranged that I should spend two nights in a flat of theirs just off Victoria Street. Further study of the foibles of my future colleagues and seniors seemed hardly necessary, but I was shown a good deal of additional background material, much of it (as I discovered later) almost entirely fictitious. The chief diversion was, however, provided at night. The flat contained two bedrooms, in the other of which a French couple was staying. Both nights were disturbed ones for me, because of an almost continuous quarrel, punctuated by various bumps and thumps, from next door. I mentioned this tentatively in the office, and the reason became clear: the French couple were colleagues as secret agents, but neither lovers nor man and wife; yet were on the point of being returned to France in the latter guise. Their stay in the flat, which was heavily bugged, was an only partly successful attempt by DDOD(I) (curiously unsubtle by the voyeuristic standards evinced in their LSF files) to acclimatize them to their new relationship.

The time came for me to leave, and I duly presented myself at RAF Lyneham in Wiltshire *en route* for Cairo. The journey that followed in a Dakota was both uncomfortable and, as I thought at the time, excessively dangerous. First stop was Gibraltar, where one could not help noticing that various ambulances and fire-engines were converging at the precise point toward the end of the alarmingly short runway where we were just about to touch down. The approach there is not an easy one at the best of times; but in our case we evidently had no undercarriage down, a disadvantage not noticed in the cockpit. At the last moment the pilot became aware of the situation and did a precarious overshoot, an operation that entailed teetering at low speed just above the masts of naval craft in the harbour. It was unnerving, but eventually we landed safely.

The next day's flight brought us to Biskra, an exotic oasis-town in the Sahara desert. Things seemed to be going very much better. Perhaps that made the crew complacent, since on the following morning, as we flew on toward Egypt, both engines of the Dakota suddenly cut out completely. There was an unnerving silence as the plane dived steeply downwards. Eventually, after too long a time for complete mental comfort, first one engine, then the other was haltingly re-started. As we regained height one of the crew came back into the cabin and, in the best RAF style, delivered the following remarks:

'Sorry about that, chaps. Someone forgot to switch the fuel-tanks over. Could have been a bit tricky, but luckily there were no air-locks.'

Well, f... you, I thought; try harder next time, mate. After that we only had to land in Cairo, where as a final gesture half of the erratic undercarriage decided to collapse, sending the plane into a semi-glissade that luckily failed to result in conflagration.

I slept soundly that night in a comfortable officers' mess, to be woken next morning by the most splendid figure of a man, coal-black, six and a half feet tall, clothed in flowing white robes and with a scarlet tarbush. Something of the sort had been glimpsed in transit at Biskra, but now I felt I had fully arrived in an incredible world of fantasy, my spirits rising accordingly. Nowadays, with foreign holidays and Christmas trips to Morocco or up the Nile, all that would seem commonplace. To a young man whose trips abroad had been confined to France and Italy it was a revelation, even more so than the dingy pyramid or two glimpsed in the distance. The railway journey up to Alexandria the next day merely confirmed the impression of an exotic and un-accountable new world. Installed in a first-class carriage, I found among my companions a haughty Egyptian gentle-man with an umbrella, who kept all would-be intruders (and there were many passengers wishing to board the train) ruthlessly at bay – till at the very last moment an enormously fat peasant lady was bundled by her family through the open window onto his (and my) knees. She was nice, but the journey that followed was an uncomfortable one.

CHAPTER 6

Joining the Levant Schooner Flotilla

The next morning I took a leisurely breakfast in the officers' mess, served by still more magnificent tribal warriors in tarbushes, then found my way to the Coastal Forces Base Office in the harbour. They were surprised to see me, despite a signal a few days before to the effect that a Sub-Lieutenant Kirk was being directed there for onward routing to the Levant Schooner Flotilla. *They* knew something about the flotilla, but were astonished to learn that anyone in London did, let alone in Naval Intelligence. As soon as I arrived in the little office I was subjected to an interrogation on how this had come about. It was generally quite friendly, since they were flattered to think that operations ostensibly under their own control were known about so far away. They lived in a separate world from that of naval warfare in home waters, and, though London seemed irrelevant in a way, it was nice to be recognized.

These people had no direct operational control over the Levant Schooners, but they knew in very rough terms where each of them was. My attention was soon directed to a large blackboard on one wall which contained a table of the dozen or so boats in the flotilla – LS (for Levant Schooner) 1, LS 3 and so on – together with columns in which positions and supposed states of readiness were recorded. A few of the craft were evidently in Beirut, the flotilla's maintenance base. Most were *up in the islands*, a phrase much repeated, in the conversation that followed, in tones in which nonchalant respect and a certain ignorance were clearly combined. 'The islands' evidently had something of the glamour, there in torrid Alex (as well as for me straight from the misty English Channel), of those of the South Seas in Joseph Conrad; and I must confess that they never lost it so far as I was concerned.

I ventured the opinion that I, too, ought to be up in the islands as soon as decently possible; and the denizens of that office were kind enough to arrange passage for me, on a large schooner carrying naval stores, as far as Beirut. I left three days later, not before becoming wholly disillusioned with Alexandrian social life and losing a week's pay playing my juvenile brand of bridge with some rich, hospitable and ruthless Alexandrian Greeks. After a brief stop in Haifa (where on a soulless cement quayside I first identified the pungent Levantine savour of carob) we arrived quite soon in near-by Beirut, then a city of the greatest charm. Fortunately the base office there knew more about the flotilla and its caiques than they did down in Alex. Three of the boats, indeed, were there undergoing repairs; two of their skippers, young Sub-Lieutenants like myself, were also around. They were Alec Thwaites and Allan Tuckey, who took me under their wing.

Among the pleasures of that city was the possibility of attendance, in one capacity or another, at 'The Mimosa' and 'Jeanette's', two extremely high-class establishments which not only catered for the carnal needs of coarse and brutal officers, French and English alike, but also served the best food available in that hedonistic city later on in the evening, when the cinemas closed and the marvellous French Officers' restaurant, 'Luculle', had finished for the night. I had nearly a week to wait for transport that would take me closer to 'up in the islands', and contrived to eat at Luculle nearly every night, sampling for the first time the Gallic delights of snails and frogs' legs among many other less exotic but splendidly prepared dishes. That did not prevent me from visiting both the Mimosa and Jeanette's, for mild gastronomic rather than more alluring pleasures, together with Alec. The girls there looked awfully nice and both establishments were tastefully decorated, Mimosa predominantly in pink, Jeanette's in a bolder combination, still much loved by the French, of green and purple. Fortunately for my moral fibre, the order to take passage up to Castelorizo (a tiny island just off the southern Turkish coast, forty miles or so to the east of Rhodes, which was used as a staging post on the way to the Aegean) was received before I could make a return visit to the Mimosa, where I was beginning to wonder whether the serious young officer should not consider sampling subtler delights than the late-evening bacon and eggs.

I returned twice during the next year to Beirut, a place that never lost its appeal. Bathing in the afternoon at the Bain Militaire, or once or twice, more daringly, after late-night parties given by members of the cultured and fun-loving Maronite families, in remoter coves; aperitifs at the delightful Hotel St George; excursions up into the hills, to the charming villages which looked down from below the cedars of Lebanon over the city and the sea – in one of them a delightful little girl seemed never to tire of throwing succulent grapes into the lazily opened mouths of myself and my companion; a trip to the noble Roman ruins of Baalbek out in the desert: these were some of the diversions. The Mimosa, fortunately, had somehow lost its appeal; on a marginally higher level Krak des Chevaliers, with Professor Dawkins' naughty inscriptions, was not at the moment easily attainable.

The naval base itself was not always so impeccable as its surroundings, one or two of the technical officers there finding it hard to resist selling off, in the nicest possible way no doubt, various of His Majesty's services and stores to subtle and persuasive Arab friends. With one of these officers, quite a senior one, who had an appropriate name that I shall change to Hammer, I had quite a tiff at a later stage, concerned with some obviously quite minor piece of equipment for my caique which I badly needed and he had promised to a contact outside. But the naval officers' mess as a whole was a pleasant place. Donald Smith who had been an instructor at King Alfred was there, and among other friends were the dental officer and (despite my earlier encounter with the Reverend Death at Lancing) the base chaplain, a popular figure called John Grinstead. He was intelligent, amusing, and eccentric; rather obviously known as the Bishop, he had the curious habit, for mysterious but certainly not prurient reasons, of conducting small parties through the extensive and picturesque brothel area, where veiled and dusky figures leant invitingly through the ground-floor windows of their little houses.

It was in company with the Bishop (who had suddenly decided that a pastoral excursion to the further boundaries of his diocese was in order), as well as with Allan Tuckey, that I took passage for Castelorizo in Geoff Whittam's Fairmile ML 354. I happened to make a record of this abortive trip two or three years later, and give some details of it now – not terribly dramatic, perhaps, but giving an idea of much of the slogging work of small-boat passage-making in the changeable weather of the eastern Mediterranean (and this boat was 112 feet long, at least, against the 35 feet or so of our operational caiques). It was also, of course, winter.

We left around noon, with two other MLs following in line astern. As far as Cyprus the weather was fine, but after a brief call at Limassol, and as we headed north-westward past Paphos, the CO muttered darkly about a dirty night. I took little notice, being preoccupied at the time with a first glimpse of Greek soil with specifically antique associations. Ancient Paphos, seen above the sandy shoreline from out at sea, lacked distinctive beauty, but then Aphrodite herself, whose shrine it contained, was represented there by a mere amorphous black tree-trunk of a statue which plainly declared her to be a local fertility-goddess, perhaps of a quite sordid kind – patroness, no doubt, of earlier prototypes of Jeanette's and the Mimosa.

A swift, streaky sunset blotted out Aphrodite and Cyprus's last headland, and a bank of grey wind-cloud in the north reminded the passengers once again that an uncomfortable night lay ahead; so we descended to the small wardroom and tried to organize our sleeping accommodation. The two ship's officers had of course their own bunks; there were two extra ones, and we tossed for them – I and the fourth passenger, an Army Lieutenant who was an expert in camouflage netting, lost and slept on the floor. We both had large sleeping-bags and laid them out so that they looked deceptively comfortable. After a quick and deeply unappetizing supper we turned in. In an hour or so things became unpleasant. The boat was by this time tossing pretty heavily and there were repeated jarring crashes as the head seas struck our starboard bow. Soon the whine of the engines took a lower pitch as reduced speed was rung down from the bridge. In the wardroom things were chaotic. Pictures, books, bottles and a metal waste-paper basket were rolling all over the deck. The Bishop and Allan Tuckey (whom I did not see again after this trip, since he was captured and murdered by the enemy not long afterwards) looked pretty comfortable in their bunks, even if the scuttles were leaking over them; but I and the camouflage expert were thrown around on the wet carpet, avoiding actual collision for the most part since we were divided by a useful stanchion. Eventually I managed to wedge myself between an overturned chair and the stanchion, which, like that on HMS Hurricane years before, became something of a friend.

Soon a heavy radio set broke adrift. The First Lieutenant had descended from the bridge and snored his way irritatingly through the disturbance. The atmosphere was definitely sultry and I realized, not without surprise, that I was feeling sick: something that hadn't happened since a force 10 gale in Hurricane on an empty stomach. So I swayed miserably up the ladder, got drenched with a half-green sea that came pelting over the bridge, then was sick, and, observing with distaste the wave-torn ocean, clambered below and fell damply into slumber.

Eventually a terrific roll dislodged my nether point of balance, so that I rolled over with the chair on top of me. The Bishop flew out of his bunk and crashed on my feet; a number of fresh things broke loose. He uttered a short prayer. For a minute we lay there while the ship gyrated heavily – for some reason we were turning and the sea was coming in on the beam; but quickly the motion eased and we proceeded along quite peacefully, which, with the occasional racing of the engines as the propellers came out of the water, confirmed that we had turned right round and now had the sea behind us. Back to Cyprus, then, and all this discomfort for nothing. I staggered onto the bridge to discover from a frustrated CO that some fairly heavy seas on the foredeck had torn up a section of the breakwater, making a hole in the deck and flooding the focs'le below to a depth of three feet. Obviously it was unsafe to continue, and this meant for various reasons that the whole group had to return. The two boats astern were flashing furiously to find out what was wrong, but I could not read their signals since dark hills of water kept shutting them off from view.

The crew were bailing out with buckets and cursing their disturbed night and the immersion of their possessions in the mess-deck lockers; we passengers joined in the chain and after an hour or so the mess-deck was more or less water-free. Already in the east a faint grey light disclosed a jagged, wave-torn horizon, and looking astern the two other craft were occasionally visible, the last one lying well back, perhaps two miles. All three boats were zig-zagging heavily as the steep following seas overtook them, picked up their sterns and pushed them to one side or the other. This rushing, see-sawing progress continued for seven more hours till we rounded the south-western cape of Cyprus and came under the lee of the island. By five o'clock that afternoon we were anchored once more in Limassol bay. A disappointing trip, and no further towards Turkey and the elusive Comaro I – that is, Commander, Aegean Raiding Forces, to whom my appointment was officially designated. Was this, I wondered, the Sunny Mediterranean (an unfair question since it was, after all, early February)?

Several days had to be spent in Limassol waiting for another ML bound for Castelorizo. Conditions there were comfortable, as they usually were in shore-based naval officers' messes. But the landscape of southern Cyprus dis-appointed me – that chalky shore was in strong contrast to the steep north-eastern coastline round Kyrenia that I was to experience later – and Limassol itself was, as it still remains, a miserable little town. It was the centre of the Keo brandy business, and rumour had it that the Keo heiress, a rather plain girl in those days but of enormous wealth, was an attainable prize for the first young British naval officer to seek her hand. Like others, I resisted the temptation, until soon another ML saw me on my way northwards.

At last Castelorizo was reached, a once-beautiful little town that had been hastily evacuated, and then comprehensively stripped by concerned British military, some months before. There was not much to do there, for me at least. The chaplain, on the other hand, rushed ashore on his pastoral visit and opened up an office in the vestry of the main church, to which for a brief period naval ratings were invited to call and meet him to discuss the state of their souls. Surprisingly quickly, however, a notice on the vestry door announced that this facility was to be withdrawn forthwith. The reason was simple. The Bishop had become curiously excited by the rusting Singer sewing-machines that were to be seen outside many of the empty houses – overlooked by previous scavengers, perhaps, or dumped outside when their weight and doubtful practicality became obtrusive. Over the three days I was there he gathered a dozen such machines and withdrew with them into his vestry, where he subjected their inner souls to skilled lubrication and repair. On the earliest returning craft he carried his booty back to Beirut, either for distribution to the more house-proud of the local courtesans or for other good purposes. Pastoral duties, he explained to me on our next (and regrettably final) meeting, had to take their due place in the scheme of things.

The Commanding Officer of the Coastal Forces base at Castelorizo was a well-known figure called Lieutenant-Commander Bill Toombs, a large man of New Zealand origin and broad interests, some of them strongly acquisitive. As a junior officer I had to pour drinks – stiff gins-and-limes for the most part – for my seniors, and spent some three hours so doing when Toombs was invited on board the ML in which I was then travelling. His conversation on that occasion had a flavour of my first evening on HMS Hurricane, or of Lieutenant Seeker in one of his frequent moods of amorous recollection. It was consoling in a way that Cas (as it was familiarly known) was not really quite 'up in the islands', although on the very edge of that glamorous region, and therefore not to be taken quite seriously; otherwise I might have been deeply disillusioned. Fortunately, in any case, I managed to arrange onward passage for myself the very next day.

It was here that my time in the Aegean, something of an epoch in my life, can really be said to have begun. Passing that night between Rhodes and the south-western point of Turkey, Cape Krio, was an indescribably dramatic and romantic experience; so too the passage back eastward, deep into the Gulf of Kos, as dawn broke and a brilliant sun began to climb the sky. After forty miles or so we eased into the deep bay of Balisu, where a couple of big base schooners and three or four small operational caiques (those that penetrated enemy waters rather than sitting in dangerously proximate neutral ones) were dispersed among minor inlets. Soon I was on my way by dinghy, with my exiguous luggage and a large RAF sleeping-bag, to LS 9, the headquarters-schooner of the legendary (to me, at least) Comaro I.

Lieutenant-Commander John Campbell, RN, the first and archetypal holder of that office, was an impressive figure. An engineer officer by training, he had been drawn by harsh necessity into covert small-boat operations after the collapse of Crete, and with Adrian Seligman was one of the founders of the Levant Schooner Flotilla. Tall, powerfully-built and dark of countenance, with a lantern jaw and generally aquiline features, he had, by contrast, a surprisingly effeminate mode of speech. The total effect, nevertheless, was of keen intelligence and strong will. He seemed to know exactly what he was doing – and what the rest of us could, and could not, do – in the Aegean, the kind of man one was happy to serve under and took care not to displease. He treated most of us in a friendly, almost avuncular, manner, as he did the Greek Captain and crew of LS 9. There were three other officers on his staff on board, including a RAF supplies officer of Maltese origin called Martin-Trigona. This was the only person who ruffled Commander Campbell's outer calm; he simply could not stand the man. Poor Martin-Trigona was an ape-like individual who had, it was rumoured, been an Olympic pole-vaulter, Campbell himself having been an Olympic swimmer. One day on board a supposedly friendly wrestling contest between these two powerful physiques developed into a more serious tussle which resulted, to the amusement of the rest of us, in Triggy being hurled over the side: no great punishment in physical terms since the water was clear, deep and blue, but a moral affront from which the flying-officer did not, perhaps, entirely recover. At any rate a certain temporary humility was implanted, in itself a distinct improvement. I did not come across him much, but many months later (as will be seen) had reason to regret that he had not sunk permanently to the bottom.

The flotilla consisted, apart from the base schooners, of a dozen or so smaller caiques – basically small Greek fishing craft – that had been acquired in various ways after the Leros débacle late in 1943 and fitted out with Army tank engines and a little concealed armament. The latter consisted of two almost useless single-shot cannon affairs which could be wonkily fixed in the bows, with a couple of Vickers machine-guns for down aft. These were normally kept concealed in the hold and took some time to rig. The boats themselves varied in size from about 25 to 35 feet in length, from 5 to 15 gross tons in weight, and were better in range than in speed: some 1500 miles for the former, some 6½ knots for the latter. I thought with a certain ruefulness of the 29 knots available in MGB 673. The caiques had, of course, their original masts and sails, still useful for steadying the roll in a beam sea when visibility was not an issue. The main advantage of these craft was that they were available and cheap, and with their solid hulls and painfully lowerable masts could lie up in near-invisibility close to the Aegean rocks. Some of their history and value was expressed much later, in surprisingly fervent language, in a belated Supplement to *The London Gazette* of 8th October 1948, being a copy of a Despatch on the un-successful attempt to occupy the Dodecanese Islands after the Italian surrender in early September 1943:

'The activities of the Raiding and Reconnaissance Forces merit special mention. When the Axis had been expelled from North Africa the Long Range Desert Group and Special Boat Squadron of the Special Air Support Regiment returned to the Middle East. As it was now necessary for them to cross the sea to continue their activities against the enemy, they were trained on the Levant coast to operate from submarines, Fairmile motor launches and coastal force craft of all types, and a force of caiques and schooners, known as the Levant Schooner Force, was formed under Commander Coastal Forces, eastern Mediterranean, manned by specially selected officers and men to work with them. These latter craft were fitted with Tank engines giving them a speed of 6 knots and an endurance of 2000 miles. With the mast down they could be camouflaged so effectually that they could not be spotted when lying close inshore.

These forces were acting over the Southern Aegean throughout the period of operations. They were the first to arrive and the last to leave, and carried out many daring and successful operations in enemy-occupied islands. There is no doubt that forces of this type, well-trained and led, can be of great value both for harassing the enemy and obtaining important intelligence.'

This refers to the operations of the force until the end of 1943. I did not join it until a month or so later, but generally speaking the aims and activities remained the same, even if the heroic days of the evacuation of Leros lay behind. Incidentally the Levant Schooner Flotilla was called 'Force', rather, in that Despatch; that is a reflexion of its rather vague and mysterious status; in any case its name was soon to be changed, officially at least, to the 'Anglo-Hellenic Schooner Flotilla' when a second group manned by the Royal Hellenic Navy was created.

Comaro I had MLs and even the odd MTB under his command as well; the smaller type of ML, the so-called HDML or Harbour Defence Motor Launch, in particular, did the same sort of job as the caiques; though for deeper penetration into the Aegean and for carrying smaller parties the caiques, which were easier to conceal or pass off, were usually preferred – if not always by the raiding parties themselves, who thought the MLs more comfortable and sometimes more reliable.

John Campbell was little less surprised at my appointment from London than they had been in Alexandria and Beirut, but accepted my arrival with stoicism and charm. At present, as it happened, no available caique needed a Commanding Officer. He therefore suggested, not at all to my displeasure (since I was content to gain a little experience in these apparently strange local conditions before setting off on my own), that I should make two or three trips as Second Officer in one of the other boats.

My first appointment, therefore, was to LS 11, a stocky Samos-built caique under the command of Sub-Lieutenant Noel Clegg, a pleasant quiet man a little older than myself. I duly rowed over and presented myself; he was rather pleased to have another watch-keeper aboard, though it made the tiny cabin (which did have two rather short bunks, however) a good deal tighter. The crew numbered five, namely the Coxswain, the radio-operator, the stoker and two seamen, and they slept in the forward part of the lightly-converted hold. Everything was very primitive; all natural functions were exercised directly over the ship's side, mostly by the bollards near the port bow, with the officer or officers tending to squat by the stern, closer to the little cabin, where one could cling onto the boom-support rail. Cooking was by primus and rations fairly basic – weevilly bread baked on LS 9, a lot of tinned sausage and Canadian bacon (both equally unpalatable), but usually with fresh eggs bought off Turkish peasants ashore, also a few fresh vegetables. Fruit was scarce, but here the naval tinned variety was acceptable. Turkish Delight, curiously enough, was often available by the machinations of Flying-Officer Trigona, though the supply dried up later when a visiting potentate noticed that one of the ratings had an enormous Turkish Delight compress strapped round his neck as a treatment for boils. This was considered a needless extravagance. Generally, however, there was no shortage of cash for running the caiques, and each of them had its own private supply of gold sovereigns aboard for necessary casual purchases, or rewards, when we were away from base and in occupied territory.

That evening Clegg, with myself in attendance, was summoned for an operational briefing. We were to sail to the island of Amorgos in the east-central Aegean and there assess local conditions and make a general survey. There was some idea of establishing a forward base there. There were said to be few Germans, if any, ashore, and they were to be captured and brought back with us. After John Campbell had finished discussing the situation (about which surprisingly little seemed to be known, or at least said) he gave Clegg his typewritten orders and asked if we had any questions. Ultimately I ventured to enquire rather tentatively whether, since there was a nearly full moon, there might not be some risk of being seen. The background to this was that in covert operations in the English Channel our agent-landing operations in MGB 673 had been strictly confined to moonless nights, or at least to hours when the moon had set or not yet risen. I have always been glad that I asked that question, even though in retrospect it appears naive and even craven, since it produced the following pregnant reply, a Campbell classic in its way, delivered in

97

his most effete tones and with heavy emphasis on the plosive consonants:

'My *dear* Kirk, *all* you have to do if you don't wish to be seen by the enemy is to Paint your caique a *Pale shade of Powder blue or Pastel Pink!*'

This was advice I was to follow to the letter when I took command of LS 12; but for the moment Noel Clegg's boat, I seem to remember, was a rather battered dark blue, and in any case there hardly seemed time to alter its colour overnight, even if Noel had wished it.

Stores were got on board for a week or so's trip, and around noon the following day we set off down the Gulf of Kos towards the Kos Channel, a gap of about 3½ miles between the north-eastern promontory of Kos and the south coast of Turkey. Since the main town of Kos, which had a heavy enemy garrison, lay close to that promontory, there was always a distinct temptation to hug the Turkish coast rather tightly for this part of the passage. The trouble was that nature had planted something called the Magpie Rock close offshore and right in our track. This large rock lay just below the surface, shallow enough to rip the bottom out of any caique but invisible when the sea was calm. Since the passage usually had to be made by night, avoiding Magpie Rock became something caique skippers were fairly keen about. Noel Clegg was as keen as any, and that night chose to go very close indeed, a couple of hundred yards at most, to the Turkish shoreline. Not surprisingly, we were soon spotted; at any rate several rounds of rifle fire were fired at us. The Turkish army, who dotted themselves round their enormously long coastline with commendable zeal, tended to turn up almost everywhere and to fire at anything in sight. I felt that we were far too close in, but we could not open the distance until the dreaded Magpie Rock, at least, was definitely astern. We motored nervously along, therefore, at full speed, while Noel concentrated on raising his own and the crew's morale by ordering the hoisting of the flotilla flag. A handsome affair with the motto 'Stand Boldly On', this particular specimen had been

Under tow.

LS 12 under sail.

99

lovingly embroidered for him by his Wren girl-friend back in Beirut. I read out this stirring injunction, in a slightly cynical spirit, as I raised the flag. Noel took great comfort, even if the crew did not seem to, and stood boldly on into the darkness. Soon the immediate dangers were past and we were heading out into the open sea, intending to skirt the island of Pserimos straight ahead and cut through the Kalymnos channel on our way westward and deeper into the Aegean.

There was a light breeze, a slight sea and quite a lot of moon. The night was surprisingly warm for winter. Now, for a time at least, one could relax. It was really delightful, even if one felt rather conspicuous. Such moments in life are rare enough, and do not usually last. Suddenly there was the most almighty crash, followed by another. Confusion reigned as it gradually became clear that we were under fire, more serious this time than a few Turkish rifles popping. The tiller was put hard a-starboard; there was a certain amount of huddling of personnel beneath the level of the gunwale. Quite soon the tiller seemed to be temporarily abandoned, and the boat went round in circles. Cautious inspection revealed nothing on the moonlit sea, until a flash on the horizon, followed by another loud crump and a distinct water-spout close by, disclosed the presence of some damnable enemy craft. There was a brief discussion about which way to turn, given that we had all of 6½ knots at our disposal. I suggested heading straight for the coast of Pserimos, which lay less than a mile away and provided deep shadow within which we had a chance of escaping further sighting. Noel decided to keep going and hope for the best, and this was demonstrated to be a successful course of action when, after a few more rounds which did not come so close, the firing stopped. Next day the German radio (as we learned later) claimed the sinking of an enemy craft north of Pserimos by one of their F-lighters (which carried a formidable 88 mm. howitzer). How they lost us, and whether they really thought they had sunk us, remained a mystery, but the result was that we kept going and reached our intended little bay in the south-eastern end of Amorgos by soon after first light.

The mast was lowered and camouflage nets were spread, both of them wearisome operations. In the end the boat looked almost invisible against the rocks; that, at least, pleased me. After a long night most of us sank into exhausted sleep. Noel was, I think, a bit perturbed by the experience; so, I can say more certainly, was I. Being spotted on the very first occasion of penetrating enemy waters had not exactly been on my Aegean agenda, even despite a certain disposition towards derring-do, and it brought home to me how very slow, vulnerable and unprotected we really were.

We spent about four days cooped up in that little bay, with very little (as far as I can remember) happening. Afterwards I greatly regretted that I did not somehow take the opportunity of having a good look round that part of a beautiful island. As it was, I spent much of the time on look-out duty, just up on the grassy hill-top above the little bay. That at least was preferable to grovelling around under the sagging and extremely dirty camouflage netting. After a day or so it became known to us that there was precisely one German on Amorgos, a sergeant who lived in the main village of Katapola some five miles along the coast. He had a radio transmitter, but it was out of action. The Greek inhabitants soon learned that we were there, and it was arranged with them to escort the German to join us on board, shortly before our departure. He duly arrived that evening, accompanied by half the village. That was not in itself surprising; what was, was that many of them were in tears. He was a kindly-looking man of mature years, evidently a great favourite. Stationed there for several months, he had been generous with his rations and was much loved by the village children. Quite what purpose he served there in his isolated glory – at least when his radio went kaput – was hard to say. At any rate it was now explained to him that he would be accompanying us on his way to a comfortable prisoner-of-war camp in Egypt, a change in his fortunes which he accepted with great dignity. In spite of language difficulties, he became almost as much a favourite of the crew, over the next couple of days, as he had been in his temporary island kingdom.

The voyage back from Amorgos to our Anatolian base was relatively free from incident. No loud bangs punctuated the night, and a waning moon made us feel less conspicuous. Magpie Rock was negotiated in disdainful calm. Back home in our beautiful Turkish bay, life was rather idyllic in the intervals between trips. There were reports to be written up, stores to be replenished from the base schooners, drying-out and washing of clothes, a general make-do and mend, boat-scrubbing and repairs to nets and rigging, and that was usually all – apart of course from catching up on sleep, reading and writing letters, comparing notes with friends from other caiques, and, even in midwinter, dipping over the side in that marvellous crystalline water.

CHAPTER 7

The Santorin Operation

Three days of relative leisure, and my second Aegean trip was under way. This time the plan was to land a party of about 15 SBS (commandos of the Special Boat Squadron) and one or two sacred Greeks (as we irreverently termed the members of the Greek Sacred Squadron, another élite formation) to attack the mixed German and Italian garrison on the spectacular volcanic island of Santorin in the southern Cyclades – the central group, that is, of Aegean islands. In addition, if any German ships were in harbour there, they were to have limpet mines attached to them, from Folbots or collapsible canoes. Two caiques were to be used, LS 11 and LS 1, commanded by Noel Clegg and Skipper Stipetic respectively; the Skipper held this naval rank (and was always affectionately known as that rather than by his Christian name Bernard), having been a Hull trawler skipper: a matchless seaman and a jewel among men. I wrote an account of this particular trip not long after the war, and this forms the basis of what follows.

The two boats, loaded down with rubber dinghies, Folbots, mortars, machine-guns, radio sets, rucksacks, 'compo' rations and fairly hefty-looking soldiers, in addition to the usual naval clutter, left Balisu Bay just before dusk. As usual, all travelling had to be done at night. By dawn next morning we had safely penetrated the belt of Dodecanese Islands and were secured along the rocks in a small bay on the south side of the little island of Sirina, midway between the southern Dodecanese and the eastern Cyclades. It had been an easy passage with no alarms and tolerable weather; though since both boats were travelling with masts down (to speed the camouflaging next morning), they had rolled uncomfortably in the long southerly swell. By full daylight the caiques were virtually invisible against the rocks under their grey netting. Sentries were posted; some of us caught up on our sleep while others walked inland to bring gifts of tinned food to the island's patriarch, Barbaiannis or Uncle John. He and his family were the sole inhabitants of Sirina, and he was a good friend to his nautical British visitors, whom he would entertain with warm goat's milk and fresh feta cheese in his stone-built hovel. Around him would sit his five sons with their wives and children, as well of course as some of the goats. Visitors were seated on rough olive-wood stools covered with thick fleeces, deliciously comfortable for about four minutes until the first batch of flea-bites started to swell. That afternoon was baking hot, and for that reason as well as the bites I soon walked up to his rather salty well for a splash around. Two small grand-sons drew the water in battered pails and hurled it at me while I manipulated the home-made olive-oil soap.

Work began again at sunset and the crews turned to and removed the nets, rolling them up and stowing them along the deck against the ships' sides – a dirty and irritating job, since as always they were full of dust. Then the heavy mast was raised in each boat with the help of collapsible steel sheer-legs. An hour later we pushed the bow out from the rocks, let in the clutch and sailed out of the bay in line ahead, LS 1 leading. At all of six and a half knots the two boats made their way slowly through calm seas, with the loom of Astypalaia to the north and Anaphi to the south. On this occasion there was no moon to speak of. By two a.m. we were well into the heart of the Aegean, which the enemy considered relatively immune from naval intrusion. Then by an hour before dawn Stipetic was leading us apparently straight into the cliff of the steep islet called Anedro, 'Waterless'. He knew the place and we followed optimistically into a narrow cleft about thirty yards wide. Engine was stopped, stern anchor dropped and LS 11 swung in toward the cliff on our port bow. The most agile of our sailors jumped onto a small ledge he had spotted and received the bow-line, which with some difficulty he grapnelled onto the rock. Ahead of us, LS 1 was equally busy with ropes; after half an hour of fine adjustment (that is, stumbling around in the dark, uttering strong oaths, slipping on the rocks or tripping over soldiers and their gear on board) we were both secure. There was a slight southerly swell lolloping inside the cleft, but nothing much, and we lay safe and snug. Then came the routine of mast-lowering and camouflage, after which watches were arranged for sentry-duty and the rest of us turned in.

At midday we came to life and a meal was prepared on the primuses. After lunch Noel Clegg and I lugged one of the heavy RAF cameras up to the top of the hill, which was about 800 feet high, and took photographs of the hide-out. Even from the hill-top the boats could scarcely be seen, so that from the air they would be completely invisible; while there was little chance that any German surface craft would be enterprising or inquisitive enough to approach too closely to such a barren rock. We felt safe and carefree as we basked in the late afternoon sun, with Santorin quite plain to see, dark violet on the horizon.

That evening, before supper, we discussed the plan of action, little disturbed by a couple of German transport planes that flew overhead on their way from Rhodes to Athens. To give a clear idea it is necessary to describe rather fully the topography of the target. Santorin itself forms a precipitous semi-circle open to the west. Part of the gap on that westward side is filled by the smaller but lofty island of Therasia, while in the centre of the interrupted circle lie two islets, Palaio and Neo Kaimeni, which form the core of the huge ancient volcano of which Therasia and Santorini form the surviving parts of the rim. Thus the two Kaimeni islets, just mounds of black pumice and rubble, each about half a mile across, lie in the middle of the vast and almost landlocked Santorin bay. The greater part of the enemy garrison was believed to be stationed in the main village, Phira, scattered along the top of the beetling purple cliffs on the western or inner side of Santorin, overlooking the great bay.

Anedro, where we were lying that evening, is some twelve miles north-east of the northernmost point of Santorin. The intention was to make for the eastern side of the main island first, landing a small reconnaissance party under the command of Stefan Kasoulis, the Greek liaison officer. This party was to approach the monastery of Perissa, which lies near the coast under the vast prehistoric rock of Mesovouno, and obtain information from the monks there about the disposition of enemy troops – it being fairly certain that this part of the coast was unwatched.

The reconnaissance party was duly landed and picked up again an hour or so later, to report that the monastery was nowadays inhabited not by supposedly well-informed monks but by obliging but slap-happy peasants, who added little to our knowledge. It was now after one a.m., and we proceeded perforce with the next part of the plan, which was to sail round the south-western tip of the Santorin horseshoe and into the great bay itself. There we proposed to manoeuvre the caiques into a deep and extremely narrow inlet on the western, seaward side of Neo Kaimeni – 'where *no* one will dream of looking for you', as John Campbell had remarked with great confidence three days before. Both our craft slipped unperceived into the bay, giving the actual headland a wide berth since there was thought to be an enemy machine-gun post by the lighthouse there. We stopped engines close to the two volcanic islets. The night was one of profound darkness, especially as the whole bay was overshadowed by the surrounding high cliffs, against which the white houses of the crowning villages could just be distinguished. The chance of navigating straight into the inlet was small, so it was decided to launch the two Folbots, one from each caique, to paddle close inshore, discover the mouth of the inlet and lead the two caiques in. Skipper Stipetic climbed into one boat, our Coxswain into the other, and they disappeared into the gloom. There followed a long wait – evidently something was wrong. Over an hour later they returned to report that they had searched the whole western coast of the islet, and that not a trace of a creek or inlet was to be found. All there was, apparently, was a small shallow indentation.

The eastern sky was already turning from black to grey; there was no alternative to lying up in this little indentation and possibly shifting the caiques later when we had reconnoitred from the landward side. Skipper in his Folbot led the way, with us following close astern, the propeller only just turning over, while LS 1 lay off till we had secured along the rocks. Almost at once, of course, we ran aground, the indentation proving to be far from steep-to. Eventually, by shifting some of the weight on deck and heaving away with poles and spars, we got clear and manoeuvred the caique another ten yards closer inshore. That was the best that could be done, and word was sent to the other craft to come alongside us. It too ran aground, but was at last in position with some three inches of water under the rudder.

It was now full daylight, and the situation looked rather gloomy; in fact it definitely put us off our breakfast. Apart from the fact that the boats were nowhere near the rocks, but separated by five or six yards of clear water, and that their sterns clearly protruded from the coastline, we now were able to appreciate to the full another alarming feature: that the rocks, instead of being the regular Aegean grey, were made of reddish-brown volcanic lava. Consequently the camouflage nets, which were dirty speckled grey in colour, were worse than useless. The sun was blazing and everyone felt tired, irritated and more than conspicuous. The only consolation was that the dark bulk of Neo Kaimeni itself hid us from direct observation from the cliff-top of the main island, although we would be in full view of ships passing in and out of the lagoon. Our masts had already been lowered, and it was decided to attempt concealment by spreading the two foresails (which happened, unlike the mainsails, to be dark tan) over the decks so as at least to break up our outline. It might have been better to try bluffing it out as local craft, but that would mean mast-raising again, so we posted look-outs and settled down to wait for evening.

I was feeling relatively energetic and set off to climb to the summit of our islet, armed with binoculars, to see if there was shipping in the bay and also to look for the missing creek. Walking was difficult on the pumice and it took more than an hour to confirm that there was indeed no creek or mini-fiord on the western side, and therefore that our chart was either out-of-date or otherwise fallacious. Then I struck directly for the summit, where the black boulders became larger and sharper, with the fissures between them leaking wisps of acrid smoke and small yellow puddles of molten sulphur.

That reminded me that I had read somewhere about the last eruption in 1926, when the outline of the core, especially of the 'New burnt one', which is what Neo Kaimeni means, had been extended by erupting lava. Here, then, was the explanation of the inlet that wasn't; and indeed as I looked down from the summit I could see that the whole shape of the islet was different from that given on our chart. Well, the chart on our base-caique, at least, should have been corrected, but it wasn't, and that was no help now. So I took an admiring but cautious look over the lava rocks at the great bay of Santorin which lay below and around me, surrounded by its rim of ochrous and purple cliffs. There was no shipping in the bay: I should have been disappointed but wasn't – we seemed to have enough on our hands already.

When I rejoined the caiques an hour later I found a third craft, a small fishing-boat, alongside. An animated and apparently carefree conversation was taking place between its Greek captain and Stefan. The former, a delightful fellow, touched on various bad habits of the occupying German and Italian troops, as well as on the vagaries of the wine-harvest, before revealing that German boats were only likely to pass our hiding-place at dawn or sunset. The garrison HQ, he added, was in a group of houses just outside Phira town, the total number of the garrison being no more than about fifty.

LS 12 under camouflage.

Sailors on Robert Ballantine's LS 3.

Plans for landing were changed. The raiding party was now to be landed some miles north of the Perissa monastery, and picked up forty-eight hours later from one of three points in the same neighbourhood. During this period the two caiques were to hide up in the Christiana Islands, south of Santorin itself and some two hours' sail to the south-west. When the details were fixed we took some sleep, feeling more secure now that the Greek fishing boat – with an intrepidity that one almost took for granted among the islanders – was keeping watch for us offshore. As evening drew on an immense supper was prepared, guns were cleaned, and the troops packed up their rucksacks and packets of explosive ready for landing. Once it was completely dark the caiques pushed, bumped and towed themselves clear of the shallows (where the sulphurous water, even in those few hours, had usefully cleaned their bottoms of weed). Engines were started and we proceeded out of the southerly entrance, then turned north under Therasia's shadow and, rounding the northern point of Santorin itself, cruised down its eastern side until dead-reckoning showed us to be off the landing beach. Cautiously we approached a flat and featureless shore, sounding all the time; the beach was found a little to the north, and at two fathoms anchors were dropped and the rubber dinghies launched. Soon the first boat-loads of soldiers were ashore, and within half an hour we wished the last of them good luck. Anchors were weighed, and after a delightfully calm and peaceful sail southward the Christiana Islands were reached just as dawn was breaking.

There, in the larger of the two (itself a mere mile in length), the two boats lay camouflaged, one astern of the other, in a steep cleft in the rocks, well protected from the north and east but still rather open to the west. That first day passed idyllically; there was plenty of room on board now that the troops were gone, and we slept and ate and wandered over the island, which had one solitary inhabitant, an ancient, jovial but slightly demented shepherd who brought his flock over from Santorin during the spring and summer months. The Coxswain and I constructed a fishing-net out of spare camouflage-netting and tried to catch some of the fat red mullet that could be seen swimming in the green depths of the rock pools. This crude effort was easily thwarted, so we dined as usual off tinned sausage, baked beans and ship's biscuit. That night we slept soundly, but just before dawn the look-out poked his head into the cabin and whispered that he could hear the noise of an engine. Noel Clegg had a look through a gap in the netting; sure enough a ghostly craft glided past, travelling westward about a hundred yards offshore. It quickly disappeared and tension relaxed. With full daylight, however, a sharp westerly breeze sprang up, making our berth distinctly uncomfortable. Our caique was in the more exposed position of the two, and Noel decided to move her into an 'ideal-looking cave' he had discovered the previous afternoon in the course of an exploratory trip in the Folbot.

Those caiques (as the attentive reader will have deduced already) were for some tiresome technical reason not equipped with astern gear, so that it was with considerable difficulty that we got clear of the old berth. Waving a temporary good-bye to the Skipper and his crew, we chugged along the coast for half a mile before Noel spotted his concealed opening, pushed the tiller hard over, put her out of gear and gave orders to be ready to bear off forrard. Slowly the caique glided into the greenest, dampest, most confining and generally evil-looking sea-cave I have ever set eyes on. It was only when we were well and truly in (by the skin of our teeth) that we realized that despite the apparent flat calm outside there was a surprising amount of swell running inside, which sent the boat into a perpetual roll and generally threw her around like a pea in a bottle. Two of the crew stumbled back to the bow with bearing-off spars, another two heaved against the sides of the cave further astern. It was an intolerable situation, one that could not have been all that easily foreseen (admittedly, Skipper Stipetic was not altogether surprised to hear about it later, but then he was a real seaman while we were amateurs). With no astern gear, and too much sea running in to make towing out by dinghy feasible, laying a kedge anchor astern was the only solution. Before doing so, since the swell appeared to be dropping slightly, we decided to wait another hour.

We all took turns at bearing off; when mine was finished I decided to combine duty (in the form of looking for a more suitable berth) with the pleasure of escaping for a while from that odious cavern. The gunner came with me in the Folbot, but scarcely had we paddled clear of the entrance when we went, as the saying goes, to panic stations; for we suddenly saw proceeding coastwise towards us, some six hundred yards away, a black German-type rubber dinghy, two of whose three occupants were staring at us through binoculars with close attention. LS 1 had no such dinghy, so I connected it with the craft glimpsed earlier that morning. Jostling back into the cavern we reported what we had seen, then loaded some grenades and a couple of Tommy guns into the Folbot before setting out again to investigate the intruder. Turning the corner near the mouth of the cave we could see that the range was now about three hundred yards, though neither side could properly identify the other because of the intervening slight swell. Smith the gunner paddled while I stared through the binoculars, nursing a Tommy-gun on my knees. Suddenly both the Folbot and the rubber dinghy hit crests of the swell at the same moment and for a split second were held there, each in full view of the other. I caught sight of an armoury bigger than ours, but also of a face I knew. Recognition was mutual; our suspected assailants were part of the crew of another British caique, belonging to another and smaller secret organization (an Army rather than a primarily naval affair) which kept annoyingly silent about the position of its various craft, and about which we had, unfairly, a rather low opinion. It was irritating, in any case, that all the decent hiding-up places in the Aegean should be cluttered up with British craft . . . Anyway, it was Captain Beckinsale and co. that had slipped past earlier; they were now lying up just round the corner and looking for a better berth for the future. We tried to decide between us who would have opened fire first; I tried

112

to entice them into our cave; and after sundry other pleasantries we parted.

Back inside, conditions were slightly improved though still hateful, and a retreat seemed feasible. The water just beyond the cave-mouth was very deep, some thirteen fathoms, which made getting any firm grip with a kedge doubtful; nevertheless two good lengths of grass line were bent onto the chain, and the two strongest of the crew rowed the dinghy out of the cave with the heavy bight of line dragging in the sea. When they could get no further they hastily manhandled the anchor overboard, while the rest of us aboard the caique started heaving in for all we were worth. The anchor held for no more than three or four seconds, but during that time the boat gathered a bit of sternway. The captain shoved the tiller hard over, and the stern swung round to port; then he let the clutch in, and with tiller reversed pushed the throttle up to full speed. It was a perilous but skilful manoeuvre, and we held our breath as the stem soared past the rocks at the cave-mouth with no more than a yard to spare. No one was sorry to leave those Stygian waters, and it was rather apologetically that LS 11 crept back into her original berth.

The rest of the afternoon passed peacefully enough, apart from some heavy explosions from the direction of Santorin. The radio link with the shore party was not working and we worried about who was winning. Everyone was glad when evening came and it was time to raise masts. But the sunset had been an ominous one, and once clear of the shelter of land we met a stiff breeze that whipped the tops off the waves and threatened to develop into a heavy blow from the north. The night was black, and time and time again we nearly lost sight of the caique ahead, which was standing up better than LS 11 to the bow seas. After much flashing with a blue lamp it was decided that we, as the slower, should take the lead and set the pace. By now both boats were pursuing a drunken course which made the danger of separation all the greater, and sure enough in another half hour contact was finally lost. We carried on, since a degree of shelter was to be expected as

113

we closed Santorin. We were making less than four knots against wind and sea; the wind, still increasing, had gone round to the port bow, and we altered course slightly to port to offset it. After three more hours Santorin did not appear much closer, but occasional glimpses through the spray and the gloom showed the high mass of Mesovouno still lying ahead. Binoculars were saturated, eyes bleared and smarting as the seas came over fairly solid now. Noel was down below trying to put a running fix onto the chart, although accurate bearings were almost impossible.

All at once we seemed to enter calmer water; I peered around, saw nothing, dried the binoculars again and through them sighted a dark patch apparently on the horizon. By dead-reckoning we were still some distance from land, but I slowed down the engine. Suddenly I realized that a flat shore-line lay right ahead; I dragged back the clutch lever and ordered hard-a-starboard, but not in time. The caique ran aground at a fair speed, but fortunately on a sandy, shelving beach. Noel rushed up from below, swore abominably, and tried to organize our removal from this predicament. It was no time for navigational inquests, but it was clear that too much allowance had been made for drift, also that we had been swept still further inshore by a coastal current from the northern headland. We had run up onto the low-lying, vine-covered plain of Perissa; the main mountain ridge lay two or three miles inland, and the low plain in front of it had been virtually indistinguishable from the surface of the sea in the prevailing conditions.

Fortunately no serious damage seemed to have been done to the propeller, though the rudder was jammed fairly hard into the sand; but although the beach was comparatively sheltered there was a sizeable swell running, and to make matters worse the wind veered and started blowing onshore. It was too rough to launch the wooden dinghy, which was small and none too seaworthy, so the big round rubber RAF dinghy was inflated and pushed over the side. I climbed in with one of the crew, and the heaviest anchor was lowered into it. A heavy anchor in a rubber dinghy, one that is already half-full of water, is not the easiest thing in the world to manage. It was a re-play, in still stickier circumstances, of the sea-cave drama. Sweating profusely, we tried desperately to paddle the yellow monstrosity into the wind, astern of the stranded craft; and then, stumbling and swaying, to tip the kedge anchor overboard before the weight of the cable pulled us back to where we had started from. Three times the anchor was dropped, but the bottom here was weedy and it failed to bite. Eventually the attempt was abandoned; meanwhile Noel had investigated forrard and discovered that she was not hard aground there. All heavy gear was moved amidships; spare fuel and water was pumped overboard; a quantity of stores was jettisoned. Then half of us (we were only six in all, apart from the helmsman) bore off with spars, while the rest were in the water shoving with might and main against the stem. Still no success.

By this time it was 4 a.m., only two hours from daylight, and the situation looked unhealthy. First, we did not know whether the raiding force was in control of this part of the island or not, or where they would be hiding during the day. Second, there had clearly been some heavy fighting, and enemy reinforcements could be expected at any time – certainly reconnaissance from the air. Third, if the raiding party happened to be in difficulties, the fact of having to wait an extra day would be a serious matter for them; although it was far from certain that evacuation would have been possible that night, even if we had not been late. So efforts to force the caique afloat were continued. Every bit of heavy gear that could be dispensed with was flung overboard, and, spurred on by the image of our trusty craft stuck conspicuously on a flat and featureless beach as a target for JU 88s, all hands made a supreme effort at kedging, bearing off and rolling the craft at the same time. Again, failure: the stern seemed to be jammed against a rock, a solitary rock sunk into a sandy bottom. It was incredible that we couldn't get the boat free, but we just couldn't. Noel and I had a rapid conference. Two things appeared essential, to get local help in towing or pushing the

115

caique off as soon as daylight came, and to contact the raiding force. It was decided that I, since I spoke a certain amount of Greek, should go ashore and try to achieve these two aims. So I strapped on a revolver , put a section of chart and a tin of corned beef in my pocket, tied a spare pair of rubber shoes round my neck and waded ashore, promising to return as soon as possible after dawn.

My first objective was a small village called Emborio which was marked on the chart as lying a couple of miles inland. Walking through those primitive vineyards in the dark – this is where the moon that had been all too brilliant on our Amorgos trip would have come in handy – was no fun at all. The soil was sandy and loose, and every fifty yards or so there was a ditch or a wall to trip over. Eventually I made out the white glow of houses, and soon entered a rough track which turned into the village street. The place seemed to be full of dogs, which barked furiously as I stumbled over some of the boulders which were apt, at that time, to encumber village streets in Greece. I prayed fervently that no patrolling or fugitive enemy troops had reached this place. Choosing what appeared to be one of the bigger of the houses, I climbed its three rough steps and knocked softly on the door; then, as there was no sound from within, harder. In the end I nearly beat the door down, and a frightened voice enquired who I was. '*Enas philos*, a friend,' I replied in the best theatrical tradition, 'who needs your help.' The door was slowly opened by an old man in a nightgown, and I stepped inside; crouching behind him was his ancient wife. They were clearly relieved that I was not in German or Italian uniform, and accepted my assurance that I was 'Inglezos' without question and with evident rejoicing. I was seated in the best chair, damp and scruffy as I was, and given a glass of harsh liqueur, which did me all the good in the world; for I had suddenly realized that I was feeling extremely tired.

Then we got down to some tortuous conversation. My Greek was not too bad at a simple level, but country folk found it difficult to accept that any foreigner could have any knowledge at all of their language, and simply would not listen or try to comprehend. That still happens in Greece even today. Gradually, however, I gathered that there were no enemy troops in the immediate vicinity. No definite news had been received about the fighting in the hill villages, though rumour had it that the garrison had been almost eliminated and that scattered remnants were wandering round the mountains in a state of confusion. It was clear that my host, while approving of the garrison being attacked, was not keen on this happening in his own village, which was understandable enough. Next I told him that our caique had run aground, and that we needed local help to get her off. Here language difficulties cropped up again, since he refused to believe that I could mean 'caique'; for it was generally assumed in the islands that British commandos, when they arrived, came in nothing humbler than a submarine or perhaps a cruiser. He decided that he must call in a young man of the village who had excellent English, and nothing would dissuade him. There was an interminable wait; eventually the young man arrived, said 'Good-bye' in polished American and lapsed into silence. I addressed him encouragingly in slow English, but he smiled apologetically and told the others that his own excellent English had temporarily deserted him. Yet he did consent to talk to me in slow and simple Greek, and gave me important news: that the raiding-party was not at the pick-up beach, two or three miles to the north, but at the monastery of Perissa itself, which lay quite close by. I accepted his offer to guide me there, and his promise that as soon as daylight came he would collect some friends and launch a fishing-boat which could drop a kedge anchor further out, or try to tow us clear.

Without delay we set off together, my companion chatting volubly as we walked along dusty lanes between the fields of vines. He was keen that we should take him with us, but I could make no promises. Just as dawn was breaking we reached the monastery, a handsome and quite extensive complex of buildings with two or three white-washed domes. It appeared deserted, but as we approached closer an English voice shouted a challenge. I replied hastily and a tired-looking sentry emerged to escort us into one of the outhouses. There I found most of the raiding party spread over the stone floor, their bodies flung into attitudes of extreme exhaustion. Against the wall were half a dozen German sailors, staring apprehensively into the barrel of a Sten gun wielded by one of the sergeants. The Commanding Officer, Andy Lassen, was awake, and I told him of the naval situation. He was not pleased. From him I learned that there had been a pretty stiff fight which ranged all over the mountains and lasted for some thirty-six hours; that two of our own people had been killed, delightful Stephan Kasoulis and the medical sergeant; the latter had just died after walking for four hours over the hills with a magazine-full of Schmeisser bullets in his stomach. This was a tragic loss, but the enemy had suffered far worse: at least thirty killed, ten captured, and the rest scattered over the island in a state of panic. The radio station had been destroyed and a complete set of confidential books and ciphers captured, but not before a signal had been sent to the mainland for help.

There was no food left, since some of the stores had had to be abandoned, so my tin of bully provided a rather scant breakfast for about fifteen hungry men. I discovered that even if we had been able to reach the pick-up beach on time we should have found no one there, for the soldiers had been too exhausted to travel further that night. I sincerely hoped that the Skipper had turned back to the Christiana Islands when we became separated. Meanwhile a signal had been sent on an Army set requesting a relatively high-speed vessel to evacuate some of the party, since it was hoped at that stage to save the sergeant's life. I promised to keep them informed about progress with the stranded caique, and confirmed that the pick-up beach for the second night was Perissa itself; then started back for the place where the caique had run aground.

By now it was full daylight and I took what cover I could. My legs were heavy and unresponsive, both pairs of shoes almost torn to bits, so the journey took almost three hours. As

I continued along the empty shore I began to think that I had miscalculated the caique's position, but round a bend in the coast I came to the exact spot. There was no LS 11, only a lot of debris in the sea from the stores we had jettisoned; while paddling knee-deep in the water were three stalwart Greek women salvaging what they could. I asked them what had become of the caique; after fervent embraces they disclosed that it had been disappearing down the coast as they reached the beach just after dawn. That eased my anxiety to a certain extent; there were no aircraft around yet, and with any luck they might reach Anedro or Christiana without being spotted. So I started back for the monastery, but collapsed into a ditch after an hour and fell straight asleep. Discomfort eventually conquered exhaustion, and an hour or so later I got going again, reaching the monastery at midday. Andy Lassen and his men were in better shape now, and relieved to hear that at least half the pick-up team was probably intact. The food situation had greatly improved, since the peasants from round about were bringing in gifts of tomatoes, fruit and cheese. An excellent fellow called Niko, who had attached himself during the fighting, was the self-appointed centre for all reports about what was happening in the rest of the island. Shortly after my arrival he brought news that two Arado seaplanes had landed in the harbour during the morning, and had recently taken off again; also that a destroyer had been observed lying stopped just to the south of the island. Nothing could be done till nightfall, so I went out with Andy Lassen to look at the remains of a little circular Hellenistic shrine that lay not far beyond the courtyard wall. It was my first sight from close to of an ancient Greek building in its natural setting, and must have been an emotional moment. Yet how far I took it all in I can't quite remember; I was feeling slightly *déplacé* by now, quite strange in fact. The afternoon sun was so hot that we fell asleep under a near-by fig-tree, to be woken by the roar of engines. Through the leaves of the tree above we saw four Junkers 88 planes sweeping overhead at about two thousand feet. They circled the monastery for a full five minutes, but

119

everything was under cover and they saw nothing; then they flew off northwards, still searching. I thanked heaven for two things, that the caique had got away and that those pilots were not extravagant with bombs, since the Perissa monastery stood out as the only obvious place of refuge on that whole coast.

It was now four o'clock, and the hours until nightfall were passed with a certain impatience. At last the whole party moved down to the beach, together with the prisoners and a handful of Greeks who had been loyal helpers and wanted to join the Greek Army. My Emborio friend was one of them. We looked for ages out to seaward, fervently hoping that nothing would prevent the caiques from showing up; the weather, at least, had abated. Just before midnight not two but three shapes were dimly discerned, two to the south and one to the north, all converging on our beach. The northern boat was a puzzle, but eventually I could identify it as an HDML, which had (it turned out later) been not far away on a different operation and had been diverted to meet the appeal for a faster

The staging-cleft on Anedro

120

craft – 11 knots against 6½. Identification signals were flashed to and fro, after which the caiques anchored a bit offshore while the ML (with its astern gear) came in closer. The prisoners were embarked first, then the rest of the party. It was a wet and rather precarious journey by dinghy, since it was still far from flat calm. There was a good deal of confusion, not least because half the male population of Emborio seemed to have turned up on the beach, in addition to the legitimate evacuees, and were climbing into the dinghies in the hope of being taken 'to Egypt'. They were reluctantly turfed out, and in the end the whole lot of the rest of us were away, about half in the ML and the remainder divided between the two caiques.

For my own part I was glad to climb on board LS 11 again and renew acquaintance with Noel Clegg and the now cheerful crew. My one day as a soldier had been too energetic for my liking, and I decided that naval life was best, even if we did run aground occasionally. Noel filled in the gaps for me. They had entirely given up hopes of re-floating the caique, and were resignedly waiting for my return with reinforcements. Suddenly and with no apparent reason she drifted free – presumably because of the infinitesimal tidal surge that often occurs in a theoretically tideless Mediterranean. They had sailed to Anedro in full daylight and with some apprehension, which would have been increased had they known that an enemy destroyer was in the vicinity. And it was there that the three craft met up again after the pick-up from Santorin. An exhausted but relatively contented day was spent in Anedro, though the shadow of the two dead men hung over us; then after a further night's journey and day's lying-up we were back at base. In spite of alarms and excursions the operation had been successful. It was not long before we learned that the German destroyer had disgorged a considerable force on Santorin the very night we left, and that these troops had spent several fruitless days searching the island. The people of Perissa and Emborio were safe, but one tragedy I learned of only years later: that the SBS had booby-trapped a church in

Phira before leaving, and that some of the villagers had ignored the warnings that had been given them and entered with fatal consequences.

One further matter about this expedition needs to be recorded, if only to help put the record straight. It concerns Anders (Andy) Lassen, the brilliant Danish SBS officer who commanded the raiders. He had joined the British Army, was already legendary for his bravery and much decorated, and was soon to die in Italy in an action that won him a posthumous VC. He was one of those people who are quite fearless and also, at times, quite ruthless, a potential *berserker*. A truly heroic figure in the Iliadic sense, the sheer force of his personality meant that uneducated Greeks could usually understand him, even though he spoke only a few words of their language. This struck me quite strongly during the hours I was with him. He was tall and blonde and intrepid-looking, but the Nazi occupation of Denmark had made him a bit unbalanced in certain respects. Thus it was that while he and his sergeant were going through the small rooms of the German and Italian barrack-building outside Phira, a couple of nights before, Lassen had ordered his companion to wake up the sleeping enemy soldiers before cutting their throats, so that they should know what was happening to them. The sergeant had refused. Nothing was said at the time, but when I met up with the party at the Perissa monastery Lassen was insisting on putting his sergeant on a charge for disobeying orders. The other officers had tried to dissuade him without much success. He told me about the incident at some length, during our leisurely afternoon together; naturally I too advised him to calm down, that the sergeant had after all been completely right. Eventually he did calm down, or at least not press the charge, but it reminded one that war was a dirty business all right.

CHAPTER 8

An Eccentric Visit to Mykonos and Elsewhere

Once again it was delightful to be back in Balisu Bay. Letters had come from home and the world seemed bright. Soon, however, life was to become more complicated. For some reason that I cannot remember LS 11 had to go down to Castelorizo, which meant that I was available as Second Officer on another operational caique. LS 12 was just off for a reconnaissance of Mykonos and Paros in the Cyclades, and Ron Taylor, its Captain, was glad of some assistance. He was a distinctly curious figure, older than the rest of us, and had been an officer in the Merchant Navy; was now, therefore, a Lieutenant RNR. It was only later that I heard he had been a patient not long before in the Royal Naval mental hospital at Kantara in Egypt, being discharged with the recommendation that he be given an outdoor job. What more suitable, some bright spark on the staff of C-in-C eastern Mediterranean had obviously thought, than the Levant Schooner Flotilla, where conditions were so noisome and confined below deck that one spent almost all one's time in the open air? Anyway, Taylor had evidently done everything that was required of him so far, probably knowing more about the business of seamanship, indeed, than the rest of us, Skipper Stipetic apart, put together.

He was a dour-looking man with a screwed-up, rather monkey-like, face, but seemed and indeed usually was quite amiable. As we set off down the Gulf of Kos once again it was clear that relations were to be more formal than with Noel Clegg, and that 'Number One', as he called me, was to do a good deal of scurrying around. I did not mind that in the least; was glad, in fact, to have plenty to do. The timing of this trip was different from that of the previous one, so that the vicinity of tiresome Magpie Rock was to be reached just after sunset. Taylor became very keen to establish our exact position about two hours before this, as we sailed quite close to Kara Ada, a conspicuous rocky island just off the entrance to Bodrum. From then on he had me taking bearings of various little Turkish headlands close on our starboard side, and on the promontories of Kos further away to port. At first I thought that these 'running fixes', which were absolutely unnecessary and almost entirely useless at this point, were merely to test my powers of accomplishing that sort of thing. Gradually I came to wonder: Taylor seemed genuinely concerned about our exact position (which was, as I say, not seriously in doubt, since we were relatively close inshore, it was still daylight, visibility was excellent, we were streaming a log, and so on). At all events I was dashing up and down from the little cabin and the chart-table, holding my hand-bearing compass, like a jack-in-a-box, while Taylor himself scanned the surroundings continuously through binoculars. I kept on reporting exact positions; Leading Seaman King at the tiller was given constant minor re-adjustments to our course, which had to be repeated in full in good big-ship style ('five degrees to port, Sir; five degrees to port it is'); the rest of the crew was kept busy doing various unnecessary things in the fore part of the boat. This was all very exhausting, and we were not yet in enemy waters. Sailing along the Turkish coast was really a completely safe occupation in these circumstances, provided one kept out of rifle range (and we were after all flying a Turkish flag for the time being); and Magpie Rock was still some way ahead. I began to put together in my mind various odd remarks, humorous innuendoes really, that one or two of the other caique skippers had made about Ron Taylor, and to wonder whether the old boy was not in fact slightly dotty.

Suddenly, unambigously and without further warning, it

was made clear to me that this was exactly what he was. He had been sweeping astern with his binoculars, in an apparently pointless but rather thorough manner; a fleeting reminiscence of Captain Howard-Johnston and the Newfoundland cod-banks came almost inevitably to mind. Then followed this question:

'By the way, Number One, did you see that U-boat sur-facing astern of us about five minutes ago?'

'No, Sir,' I replied.

'Yes, dead astern of us, about a mile astern.'

'Did you say five minutes ago?' I asked.

'Something like that, yes.'

'But you didn't mention it at the time?'

'No I did *not,*' he replied rather testily.

I reflected for a moment or two, then 'Look, Sir,' I said, 'I don't think you *can* quite have seen a U-boat, it's most un-likely there should be one knocking around here so close in to the Turkish coast.' I forebore to mention the extreme eccentricity of not mentioning such a major event, if it had actually occurred, for a full five minutes.

After another long silence Taylor said, 'You will kindly send off an enemy report *at once.*' Further discussion seemed out of the question, so I dashed off a brief signal for C-in-C Alexandria, repeated to Comaro I, reporting the sighting of an enemy submarine just south-west of Bodrum, then gave it to Sparks for coding and despatch. Fortunately John Campbell, at least, as Comaro I, tended to be cynical about this sort of information, and in any case there were no naval resources around to be sent scurrying off at that moment after phantom submarines. I reported to my Commanding Officer that the signal had been sent and he grew calmer. In fact by the time we approached Magpie Rock, and as darkness fell, he steered past it in a very relaxed manner.

After a first staging-stop at Sirina (described in the pre-vious chapter) we headed north-westward to reach 'Stapodhia' before dawn. This was the Admiralty chart's Italianized name for a conveniently barren islet called Khtapodhi or Octopus, which lay just to the east of Mykonos. The day was spent under nets. On the third night we landed our little raiding-force party (one SBS officer and two other ranks) in one of the eastern bays of Mykonos itself. By this time the wind had increased a good deal, and Ron Taylor decided to wait out the night there at anchor. The mast was left up, and we were to pass for a Greek caique so far as all enquirers were concerned. There was thought to be a small German garrison ashore, but they were over on the other side of the island, some ten miles away, in Mykonos town; moreover rumour had it that they were scared stiff about British raids, and spent as much time as possible barricaded in their quarters.

When dawn broke there was a northerly gale blowing, and we had to double up the anchor; Taylor decided to stay where we were. This gave the two of us a good deal of time for conversation down in the cabin. He evidently needed to discuss many of his ideas and feelings, and I learned for instance that it was his intention to spend part of his life after the war helping in a leper colony. I did not entirely believe him, although I later heard that he carried out the intention. A truly estimable man, unusual in many ways, though at the time I would have preferred a Commanding Officer who was a good deal saner. Talking to me – it was something of a monologue – seemed to relax him a great deal. As the afternoon drew on, however, he became visibly restless. Eventually he decided to take a walk ashore in disguise, as he put it, and gather some information. What kind of information was not clear, since in any case he spoke no Greek. He had noticed that I had with me a pair of grey flannel trousers (most of us tended to wear informal civilian clothes on board, usually a sweater and shorts, just keeping a symbolic naval cap at hand in case of trouble – a waste of time as Allan Tuckey's capture and subsequent execution demonstrated). These he borrowed, and proceeded ashore carrying one of the ship's buckets. He said he looked like a milkman. Quite soon he returned on board, having met nobody and seen nothing except a lot of Greek island scrub and some good views of the coastline.

Another night passed, the weather eased, but Taylor decided to wait where we were: he was dead keen on having a longer excursion ashore in his disguise.

This time he was gone for several hours, during which I had visitors. A small party of Greeks, including a tall and heavily-bearded priest in full rig, appeared at the head of the bay and made urgent signs for someone to go and talk to them. I rowed ashore in the dinghy and found the priest to be a very grandiose figure, the Abbot in fact of the island's monastery at Tourliani. He was also, according to him, head of the local resistance. Later I learned that he was also a considerable villain, and that all the orphans he claimed to be sheltering in the monastery had run away, quite recently, in the middle of the night. I called on him at the monastery after the war and he was extremely aggressive, blaming me for not getting him some kind of medal as well as that archetypal reward at the time, 'a block of flats in Athens'.

Anyway, after the establishment of credentials, which was done with reasonable courtesy, he suddenly became excited, indeed almost speechless with rage. His visit, it transpired, was due to Ron Taylor's capering around as a milkman. The whole island, it appeared, was whispering about this eccentric foreigner who carried a bucket around and tried to engage passers-by in a language not their own. The Abbot urged me, as a British officer, to get hold of the madman and confine him on board. Otherwise, he claimed, the Germans would hear about things and investigate not only our caique but also the goings-on at the monastery. Well, that all sounded quite logical and I replied that when my *kapetanios* returned I would persuade him to go no more a-roaming. The Abbot kissed me on both cheeks, an intensely prickly experience – incidentally he smelled heavily, not of garlic as is traditionally the case, but of rose-water – and, with his rather seedy-looking lay henchmen, disappeared up the track leading away from the beach.

When Taylor re-appeared and called for the dinghy to pick him up from ashore I went to fetch him myself, and explained that his disguise, even despite my grey-flannel trousers (which had been annoyingly ripped about during his peregrinations), had been widely penetrated. I tried to soften the Abbot's message, without hiding the fact that further milkman trips were to be avoided at all costs. There was some slight additional implication that the grey trousers, an essential part of the conception, would in any case not be on offer. Taylor seemed downcast but said little in reply. We were due to pick up the raiding party that night, in another bay a little to the north, and there seemed no opportunity for further explorations.

In the event the rendez-vous did not take place till a night later, owing to a confusion on the chart about the names of the bays down the east coast of the island, and there was another whole day to be whiled away. Milkman duty was evidently forgotten, but in the early afternoon further signs of eccentricity were displayed. Most of what then took place was observed by myself from a distance, since I had rowed myself ashore again to escape from a distinctly claustrophobic atmosphere on board, as well as to talk to, and seek information from, a couple of local characters who were languidly beating an octopus against a neighbouring rock. Suddenly, as I was chatting with them, a plane flew close overhead. It was, unmistakably, an RAF Beaufighter. These planes used to carry out occasional reconnaissance flights over the central Aegean, and indeed we had a complicated recognition system (involving one of the crew mucking about with a bucket on the foredeck) for their benefit, a system of which I later learned that they were entirely ignorant. Usually the Beaufighters flew in pairs, and evidently on board the caique some kind of argument had broken out. I could not hear exactly what was being said, but Taylor was throwing his arms around and shouting at the crew. I decided to get back on board and see what the trouble was. As I approached in the dinghy a second Beaufighter flew over, but I was more interested in the words shouted to me by my Commanding Officer:

'Number One, we have a mutiny on board.'

128

'A *what*, Sir?

'A *mutiny*, Number One.'

'Aye aye, Sir,' I replied in correct naval language, taking a close look at the crew, who were up on deck, all five of them, lounging around and appearing deliberately unconcerned. They could, of course, hear everything that was said by their Captain.

'The men,' Taylor continued, 'have flagrantly disobeyed an order from me to abandon ship and swim ashore.'

I glanced at the Coxswain, Leading Seaman King, an extremely sound character, who simply said, 'We told him it was just a Beaufighter.' Further enquiries from both sides revealed that Taylor, not having seen the plane properly, had assumed it was a German fighter and that our craft had been spotted. He had then told the crew to jump overboard and swim to the shore, some fifty yards away. It should be reiterated, perhaps, that relations between crew and officers on those boats were normally rather informal – after all, we were living at very close quarters. Also the caique crews were often a fairly tough bunch (several seamen on other boats, though not LS 12, having volunteered from naval prisons); so on this occasion someone had simply said, 'It's a bloody Beaufighter, skipper, don't panic.' Taylor had then become quite huffy and repeated his order, at which the crew had evidently gone about their business and taken no notice. They did not like swimming, in any case – indeed one or two of them, like many sailors, were likely to be incapable of it.

After one or two further mutterings about mutiny I managed to get Taylor into the cabin and persuade him to calm down. He became extremely depressed, almost tearful. Then I had a chat with the Coxswain and agreed that the incident was at a close. Finally, after sunset, we weighed anchor, picked up the reconnaissance party and started off homeward. Lieutenant Betts, the Army officer, enquired tenderly how things had been. He had already observed that Taylor was not quite himself, having been in the background during the phantom U-boat sighting incident. Now I gave him a brief and fairly jokey account of the great Beaufighter scare. That night on our voyage back towards the Turkish coast we passed fairly close to the southern shore of Samos, and contrived to give a final twist to a less than completely tranquil trip by setting fire to a large mat with which we were trying to conceal the showers of sparks that were issuing from the exhaust-pipe on our port side. The mat had been ingeniously wired on and could not be cut adrift for several minutes. Being seen by the enemy garrison ashore – Samos was quite heavily occupied and presumably had the odd E-boat available – was an annoying possibility, but Taylor (who had, I think, dreamt up the mat idea) seemed to take no further interest in proceedings. In fact he remained down below in the cabin, except for two brief occasions when he came up on deck, took a quick look through the binoculars and announced, 'I can't see a bloody thing,' after which he retired once more to his bunk. Indeed by now he seemed to regard himself as no longer in command and left things entirely to me, which suited me well enough.

Back in Balisu Bay, things took their usual course for a time. One washed, shaved, bathed, rested, read letters that had arrived during the nine days we had been away. Then a friend of mine, Jack Charrington, an Army Captain who was both caique skipper and, temporarily, on John Campbell's staff, paid me a visit on board; Taylor had been absent somewhere for two or three hours. I chatted with Jack about our trip, without mentioning, for the moment at least, my Commanding Officer's vagaries. I was wondering what to do about that, but postponed any immediate decision. Then Jack, an old Etonian who as it happens had exquisite manners on all occasions, mentioned with a courtesy and solicitude that were unusual even for him that I was to depart that very night with an MTB heading down to Alexandria. I was, of course, extremely surprised, not being due for leave, and even in my rather exhausted condition managed to conclude that something was up.

'Hey!' I said, 'has Ron Taylor been saying something about me?'

'Well, Geoffrey, he *has* mentioned to John Campbell that you've had quite a lot of seatime lately, the old nerves naturally get a bit frayed and you might rather welcome a brief rest . . .' – at which point I exploded.

'Look,' I said, 'I've been cooped up for nine days with an absolute maniac (about whom you lot must have had your suspicions), and you're going to believe that *I'm* the dotty one? Just ask the Coxswain about Ron's goings-on, or better still ask Lieutenant Betts – he's seen some of them, at least.'

Jack instantly seemed to be persuaded, and, looking rather relieved, rowed back to LS 9 to report an interesting new perspective. There, it seems, he coincided with the arrival of Lieutenant Betts, who after a preliminary report and a quick wash and shave on the SBS base-yacht, had rowed over to tell Comaro I exactly what he thought of recent events on board LS 12. The consequence, to put it briefly, was that it was Ron Taylor who left that night on the MTB, while I stayed put and took over command of LS 12.

We met up again a few months later in Chios, where a regular base had by then been established. Ron was there, and ecstatically happy, having been placed in command of the local brothels; evidently the recommendation for constant fresh air had been waived or forgotten. He was very systematic about the whole business, visiting, it appeared, every brothel every evening. The girls had all been issued with naval pay-books that had to be stamped by one of the local doctors each week, after a medical examination. Ron seemed to bear me no ill-will, in fact treated me as an old friend, and invited me to accompany him on his rounds one evening. I thought this was some kind of joke, but he was so offended that I gave in.

It was, as might be expected, a very nasty experience, worthy of the pen of a Dickens or a Lawrence Durrell. On the whole it was I, rather than those more actively engaged, who averted my eyes and thought of England. As well as being sordid, it was dangerous to boot. That is to say, Ron behaved like a complete maniac, barging into all the rooms without warning and demanding to see stamped paybooks whatever

131

the state of engagement within. Some of the naval clientèle were fairly tough customers, but on this occasion, at least, they confined themselves to uttering dire threats more or less under their breath, and I did not blame them. Presumably they did not know, or did not in the circumstances care, how close they came to a charge of mutiny. Taylor did not appear to derive any erotic *frisson* from these intrusions, but was (I believe) simply obsessed over the proper working of what was no doubt an admirable system, much of which he had personally adapted to local Chiote conditions.

CHAPTER 9

Unexpected Events in Turkey
and the Cyclades

Taking charge of LS 12 (a Samos-built caique, incidentally, twelve tons gross and originally named Maritsa) brought an entirely different feeling to my life in the Aegean. Within obvious limits, I was now free to do things the way I thought best, and that made everything easier. It was like being in the driving seat of a car; one is not necessarily a better driver than the passenger, but at least one thinks one is, and does not feel frightened. Certainly things went more straightforwardly in most respects, though that may have been largely a question of luck. At first, however, there was a frustrating mechanical problem. LS 12, like one or two of the other boats, had chronic stern-gland deficiencies (perhaps due to the weight of the Tank engine and consequent flexing of the after-part of the hull), and that meant taking her back to Beirut. Then when we had done that, and got nearly back to the Aegean, beyond Castelorizo on the way north-westward, the wretched thing started first over-heating and then leaking heavily again, so much so that I very nearly had to beach the vessel on the southern Turkish shore. Strangely enough there were no approved facilities for repairing it closer than Beirut, which had botched the job in the first place; so it was back there again – a weary haul.

Over a month of that midsummer was wasted, but at last by July 10th we were in relatively good working order and back in the area of operations: in Losta Bay, a deep Turkish inlet in the gulf of Doris just across the water from the enemy-occupied island of Symi, on which a relatively large-scale British attack, involving a couple of hundred troops, was just about to be mounted.

The day before the landing I contrived to steer the boat over a shallow inshore reef – something Ron Taylor would not have done – and stove a plank in; there was no time for refinements, so we put the boat lightly ashore on a sloping beach and energetically careened her so as to be able to apply a canvas patch. That worked pretty well, except that the upper strakes were far from watertight and we took a good deal of water aboard, causing minor damage to personal possessions. Kit-claims, properly exaggerated, were filed for this in due course. By evening we were ready to go, and took on board Lieutenant Betts-Grey (distinct from Lieutenant Betts) and five other ranks of the SBS. By midnight we had landed them on Symi, and over the next four days did a great deal of ferrying of troops to and fro, for assembly and reinforcement in Losta and the neighbouring bays. By the 15th we were in Symi again, this time in the main harbour as darkness fell. The fighting was over and the enemy garrison had capitulated, though poor Betts-Grey had been badly wounded in the process. The caiques and MLs ferried the troops and prisoners back into Losta and Penzik, then my immediate task was done and I continued on my way round Cape Krio and into the Gulf of Kos to our main operational base at Balisu.

There was a day or two in which to strengthen the stove-in plank underwater, then it was time to pick up a small group of Sacred Greeks – always good company – from their base schooner *Eliki*. The destination was quite close by, Kos itself, where they were to make a reconnaissance well up the coast from the heavily-occupied main town. The mast was lowered for the short ten-mile crossing from Mersinjik on the facing Turkish coast, where we had secured alongside the rocks in the early afternoon. The point of this was to reduce the likelihood of being seen, but the result was heavy rolling and, more serious, interference with the magnetic compass from part of the steel rigging of the mast, which as it lay along the deck had been secured too close (I concluded later) to the compass itself. In any case the magnetic environment of the boat had been altered, and I did not try making passage with lowered mast on subsequent trips after the Kos ones. Eventually I was able to correct our position by using the hand-bearing compass as we approached the mountainous coast, in a choppy sea just after moon-set and shortly before midnight. We anchored in four fathoms, and the reconnaissance party was rowed ashore. They had to make their way further up the coast for half-a-mile or so, but the dinghy eventually found a safe landing place, returning to LS 12 after what seemed a long one and a half hours.

By the time we reached Mersinjik again the radio transmitter had succumbed to dampness or motion or both, so that meant returning to Balisu instead of waiting in peaceful isolation till the Kos party was due to be picked up three days later. By the morning of July 26th the transmitter was repaired, but then there were further complications. Later that afternoon all our boats in Balisu Bay had to move out in a hurry, since a large forest fire, deliberately started (as was found later) by the Turks in order to discourage our illegal presence there, was choking us with smoke and threatening the petrol carried in one of the large schooners for the occasional MTB. It was only a question of moving into Port Deremen (another beautiful and empty bay) a few miles further to the east, but it was a nuisance. At first light next day I left them to sort things out in the new bay and motored down the south side of the gulf back to Mersinjik. By nine that evening the mast was lowered once more, and we slipped and proceeded. From Mordala islet abeam course was set at N75W for the rendez-vous beach in Kos, the sea moderate becoming rough. Closing the original rendez-vous position, we then steamed slowly up towards C. Phuka at about half-a-mile offshore. The mountain loomed directly overhead, the night was splendidly dark, and just after midnight blue flashes from ashore showed where the little party was waiting. The anchor was dropped and the dinghy sent in to fetch them; they had an extra Greek in tow.

After that it was straight back to Deremen, where a hearty breakfast was taken at the end of a simple small-scale operation, described in some detail simply because it was the first (since the Symi affair was untypically large and closely organized) that was carried out, on the naval side, more or less at my discretion. It was still too close to base to give the full sense of freedom and independence that the following months were to bring. Incidentally it was after this little trip that I followed John Campbell's classic piece of advice and had LS 12 painted 'a Pale shade of Pastel Pink'. It looked a bit unusual in daylight, but by God it was practically invisible in the dark!

A couple of days later I was given another little task quite close to home. This was to sail over to Bodrum, the sizeable harbour town, dominated by its fine Crusader castle, on the north shore of the gulf of Kos. (As Halicarnassus it was the site of that semi-monstrosity, one of the ancient Seven Wonders of the World, known as the Mausoleum.) There, some German soldiers who had somehow become an embarrassment to the Turks were to be smuggled out into British hands. Apart from being lightly shot at by a couple of trigger-happy soldiers as we approached, arrival in Bodrum just as darkness fell was relatively straightforward. Then we had to wait around for a day, keeping the boat more or less out of sight which was not always easy, since orders for the release of the prisoners had, like most such orders in Turkey, been delayed. The local British agent, a cultured and respectable-looking man (complete with panama hat) of partly Greek origin, kindly invited me to have a drink with him in town, which he said would be quite safe. As we sat down in the main cafe he indicated a group of four men in civilian clothes at a near-by table. These were the Germans in question, who had been fed a story that they were being ferried off to Kos and safety in a specially provided motor-boat. They looked quite care-free, I must say. Next afternoon we proceeded to an agreed position just off the tip of Kara Ada island, outside Bodrum bay, and hung around until nearly midnight to rendez-vous with Paradeisos's little caique – he being my host of the previous day. It duly turned up and was ordered to stop; we drew alongside it, a couple of our sailors jumped aboard and opened up the cabin. The poor Germans slowly emerged, covered with blankets with which they had been trying to conceal themselves, and very disappointed indeed when I told them in atrocious German that we were a British vessel and they would not be going to Kos after all. As usual my sailors were kind to them and gave them cups of tea, re-assuring them that life in a prison camp in Egypt was no bad thing. Their own boat returned to Bodrum and we were back in Deremen by dawn the next day.

After this harmless Graham Greene-ish diversion it was time for more serious business: a reconnaissance of Paros and Naxos in the central Cyclades which was to last for the best part of two weeks. We set off in company with LS 1 under Skipper Stipetic, heading for our by now familiar staging-post Sirina. Apart from a bit of tracer from the island of Nisyros *en route* it was an uneventful trip, and by 4 a.m. both boats were secured alongside the rocks in the south bay. Masts were lowered and camouflage nets laboriously spread; it was not long before another caique, an Army intelligence affair under the command of our old friend Captain Beckinsale, was found anchored nearby. After that the day passed in the usual hot, dusty and frustrating fashion under nets; but at least I could encourage Stipetic to go ashore and accept, on behalf of both of us, the hospitality of Barbayiannis, the island patriarch, whose nectar of steaming goat's-milk, drunk out of fetid wooden bowls, I literally could not stomach.

As darkness came we painfully stripped off the netting and raised the mast – that took an hour or so; by three the next morning, after another easy passage, we were searching for a suitable hiding-up place on the southern (and more protected) shore of Anaphi, a mountainous and under-populated island north-east of Santorin – for which Stipetic was bound once again, with me due to head up to Heraclia in the group of small islands to the south of Naxos. The trouble was that this southern coast of Anaphi was distinctly difficult; the chart revealed two likely-looking if shallow bays, but both of them were bedevilled by off-lying rocks. Memories of Santorin, also in company with Stipetic, arose, though the present situation was much less drastic. After an hour I found a rather unsatisfactory billet in a third indentation, with the Skipper near-by. A rough camouflaging job was done as the weather slowly deteriorated, and after breakfast LS1 moved off in search of something better; by mid-day I was forced to follow suit. Conditions were really quite awkward by now, with gusts of wind whipping up spray under leaden clouds; I anchored off some rocks, managed to get the stern in with a grapnel, then was still bouncing about too close to the rocks, came away from them and – of course – could not get the wretched anchor up. The thing was firmly jammed on a rocky bottom, and nothing the crew could do succeeded in prising it free. Lack of astern gear at such moments was especially constricting, and I was forced to abandon the anchor and a certain amount of chain.

Fortunately my habit of having at least two spares on board (which is where a gold sovereign or two came in useful with Greek fishing caiques we encountered) meant that we could afford to do so – but the trouble was that we immediately got into similar difficulties on the other side of the same bay. Unfortunately the Skipper was able to see what was going on from the only decent berth in that bay, and derived much legitimate amusement (not shared by me or my crew at the time) from my amateur fooling around with anchors. This time we had at least attached a thin line to the fluke of the anchor and managed to jerk the thing loose when it got stuck; but it was a frustrating afternoon, and I was relieved to be able to get the mast up after a cold and blowy supper on deck. Anaphi is a relatively unexciting place, devoid of visible antiquities (although one of the most famous of archaic *kouroi*, the Strangford Apollo, was found there) and without much merit as a port of call even in favourable conditions. I gave it a wide berth in future. That night we sailed up past Anedro and into a far gentler place of refuge, Pegadhi bay in the low and grassy little island of Heraclia, which was to be our base for the next few days.

By now it was 3.30 a.m. and the usual routine took over: down mast, on with camouflage nets, set an observation post ashore, then some sleep and a late breakfast. In the middle of the morning a couple of MO4 agents came aboard, also an amiable local inhabitant called Manolis. He was a young man of faintly spiritual appearance who had, in fact, spent some time in an Orthodox seminary. He lived with his parents and brothers in a shack-like dwelling a mile or so up the hill, looking after a few goats, and was anxious to be as helpful to the English as he could. He had already met Robert Ballantine, who had staged there earlier with LS 3. Later when I returned to Pegadhi bay he tried to get me to take him away with me, but I didn't think he would make good military material; he was, however, a great talker, and like Robert I tried to help him after the end of the Occupation (without, I think, much success). That night we landed our party of Sacred Greeks at the head of a small bay on the south-western corner of Naxos, then returned to find that the wind had increased so much as to make camouflaging in Pegadhi bay impracticable for the time being. I therefore left the mast up, flying the Greek and Occupation ensigns, and from this time on more or less gave up the idea of camouflage when in the Cyclades. It took so much out of the crew in terms of fatigue, both in the wearying processes of lowering and raising the mast and spreading and re-folding the nets, and then in the stooping, shuffling, dirty business of passing the next day under the nets themselves. There were plenty of Greek caiques lying around in those central Aegean islands, doing a bit of fishing by day and obviously protected to some extent by the special pennant, a simple red and white affair, that was issued by the Germans to *bona fide* fishing boats. There seemed no reason why we should not pass as one of them. At least that avoided those awkward few minutes (more than once chosen by a German aircraft to pass overhead) when the nets were half on and half off.

Next night it was the turn of Paros. Another little commando group was landed in a remote bay in the south of the island; then back again to Pegadhi. A day later we picked them up; it was blowing hard into the rendez-vous bay around midnight, the anchor dragged as we waited, the caique nearly blew ashore and yet *another* anchor, together with a useful length of grass line, had to be abandoned to the deep. The following night it was back again to Naxos to pick up the shore party from there. Boxes of food for the islanders were landed at the same time, after which we made course for the dramatic cliffs of Anedro for staging on the way home. In the by now welcoming cleft in the rocks there we found to our surprise a civilian Greek caique, from the island of Kalymnos; but there was of course room for two. Next evening we left early, after supper, but a force 7 northerly forced us back into shelter by 10 p.m. For two further days that wind persisted, and LS 12 lay uncamouflaged against the rocks.

Time passed more pleasantly than one might think. The Kalymnos caique, of all things, was carrying a cargo of good strong red wine; its crew were extremely friendly, opened up keg after keg of their cargo, and a more or less continuous party took place. Next day some of us climbed up the cliffs on a hunting trip: meat was needed, and Anedro contained its own particular brand of wild goats. There were about twenty of them, and they were soon scurrying for shelter on the bare top of the island, less than a mile square. An agreement had been reached between us that only single shots were permitted, but it was not long before one of the Greek officers became carried away and blazed off with automatic fire, driving one of the prey headlong over the cliff and felling another. The rest of us had scattered in panic almost as far as the goats, but eventually re-assembled and carried the dead animal down. It was skinned and butchered in no time; the Kalymnos Greeks were adept at that kind of thing, as was our Stoker Peckham. A huge fire was kindled and a great meal prepared on the rocks against which the two caiques were lying. That final celebration of allied good-

140

will lasted far into the night as the wind whistled high above us.

At last on the 14th it became plain that the storm had abated and we could be on our way. Somehow the batteries, like ourselves, were suffering from a hangover and needed a couple of hours of recharging, which made us late into Sirina, our next staging-post – well after dawn, in fact, so that we were able to recognise our old friend the MO4 caique 'Constantinos' lying there as we approached. MO4 used Sirina a great deal, often breaking down there. Anyway, 'Constantinos's' engine was feeling unwell, and we took her in tow later that evening as we headed towards Cape Krio and the Turkish coast. The tow parted twice, and our exhaust, again choked with carbon, caught fire once again, but otherwise it was an uneventful night, especially when the other boat got some response out of its engine and asked us to slip the tow. We were back in Deremen before midday, after thirteen days away, with only thirty gallons of fuel remaining. It had been a trip without major panics, give or take an anchor or two, but a completely successful one from the intelligence-gathering point of view.

After four idyllically peaceful days in Deremen, during which the engine was de-carbonized and sundry other minor repairs carried out, I was given new sailing orders, this time for a variety of islands including Mykonos, Tinos and Andros – still in the central Aegean, which I was beginning to feel that I knew, in the dark at least, almost like the back of my hand.

It may be of interest to set out here the Sailing Orders for that trip. They show (among other things) how much latitude individual caiques and their raiding or reconnaissance parties were allowed in achieving their objectives. These were themselves sometimes stated in very vague terms. In this particular case there seems to be some confusion, in addition, between northern and eastern Cyclades, but everyone knew what was meant. (It should be added that John Campbell was temporarily down in Alex; also that LS 12 was now officially called AHS 12, since a Greek-manned flotilla had just been formed and ours was officially re-named the 'First Anglo-Hellenic Schooner Flotilla'.)

From: COMARO I TOP SECRET
Date: August 20th, 1944
To: Commanding Officer, AHS 12

Subject: Operation R 15 (Northern Cyclades)
1 OBJECT To carry out general reconnaissance of the eastern Cyclades group, including Mykonos, Syros, Tinos, Andros, Jura and Rheneia
2 METHOD Your orders are open but it is essential to work in complete agreement with the S.O. GSS. It should be possible to obtain good information by landing on 2 or 3 of the islands only. If in doubt signal me for instructions.
   Embark 6 GSS, 1 Intruder, W/T
3 PROCEED STAPODIA
      ETD Deremen 1200/20
      ETA Pharlah 2359/20
      ETD Pharlah 1600/21
      ETA Themina Dawn/22
      ETD Themina 2100/22
      ETA Dragonisos Dawn/23
   Carry out general reconnaissance. Duration should not exceed five days. It should be possible to obtain good intelligence on Syros from caiques visiting Mykonos, also on Andros from Tinos, without actually landing. There is reputed to be an RDF German caique in Agios Ioannis bay, Tinos, which should be liquidated if possible.
4 RETURN DEREMEN by same route. ETA August 30th.
5 INTELLIGENCE. Mykonos, Delos, Andros are occupied. Jura, Tinos and Rheneia are not occupied. Read latest intelligence in Ops room before leaving.

6   W/T. SOP 425 kcs. LVG routine. Report all movements
    and intentions each day.
7   RETURN. It is essential to return on or before August
    31st.

(signed) COMARO I

This time our route out lay further to the north, which had
interesting consequences. Incidentally it seems to have been
changed, subsequent to the Sailing Orders above, which are
obscure in any case over what was to go on between
Stampodia (or Octopus, a favourite resort in the eyes of
Comaro I but not in mine) and near-by Dragonisi. Anyway,
we carried seven members of the Greek Sacred Squadron
(GSS) on board, four of them officers, as well as their rubber
dinghy (Intruder) and a quantity of food for the islands. On
the evening of August 20th I dropped anchor in Aspat bay,
about four miles beyond Bodrum, where it was noted in the
log that the Turks were exceedingly friendly; perhaps the
benign influence of my agent friend in Bodrum extended so
far.
    That night and the following morning were spent there.
The next port of call was rather different. It was decided to
anchor for the following night some thirty miles up the Turkish coast, in a shallow sandy bay about 2½ miles east of
Cape Monodendri ('Lone-tree') at the northern edge of the
Mandeliyah gulf. For some reason the patrol had to waste a
bit of time before arrival in Mykonos, and it was better to do
this, we thought, in the relative safety of Turkish waters. The
bay was peaceful enough and the weather calm, so I was
taking supper down below with the senior Greek officer, who
was sharing my little cabin. It was a very pleasant occasion.
Suddenly there was an almighty crash as a rifle bullet em-
bedded itself in the woodwork just above my head. I needed
no further invitation to hasten up on deck. At the head of the
bay, only a hundred yards or so from where we lay at anchor,
two characters with rifles could be discerned crouching behind

143

a rock. I waved my arms at them and shouted angrily. They took no notice, or rather they shouted angrily back. Eventually one of them emerged and made gestures that plainly indicated I should come ashore. There seemed little point in arguing, since they could shoot at us from behind good shelter and we were fully exposed if we tried to prepare the boat for leaving. Moreover, being in neutral waters in daylight, we had nothing rigged in the way of weaponry. So the dinghy was pushed overboard and I got into it, together with my Greek officer friend who spoke not only good English but also, it transpired, adequate Turkish.

As we landed, two fairly desperate-looking soldiers emerged from behind their rock. The younger one was a corporal; the other, old enough to be my father, a private. We explained that we were waiting for minor engine repairs to be completed, and would be delighted to leave in an hour or so. The corporal asked what the devil we were doing flying a Turkish flag; this seemed to annoy him, although I explained through my Greek colleague that it was intended as a courtesy, which was not entirely true. In any case, he was unimpressed. I then suggested that one or both of them should come aboard, where we would contact their higher command in Ankara on our radio and obtain confirmation that we had permission for our visit. This was a traditional ploy (involving a charade with the transmitter and the pulling of totally fictitious messages out of the ether) which, incredibly enough, normally worked with the zealous but usually illiterate Turkish militiamen. Unfortunately these two were of a different calibre, and the invitation aboard was rejected with contumely.

The older one was then despatched inland by the corporal, who kept us carefully covered with his rifle. In twenty minutes he returned, accompanied by an officer on a large white horse. We repeated our story to the officer, who seemed unimpressed. After a few minutes he told us that we had to follow him to his headquarters some three miles inland. There was little alternative, so I shouted across to the men on the caique that they should await our return. Then Yiannis (the Greek

Lieutenant) and I followed the rider and the two soldiers across the sandhills and along a rough track leading inland. The terrain was uninteresting and relatively hard going. I indicated to the officer that he ought to give me a lift on the back of his horse, but he declined. As we proceeded, the older of the Turkish soldiers kept addressing his officer in distinctly surly tones; after a time a thoughtful-looking Yiannis vouchsafed the news that he was trying to persuade him that we should be peremptorily disposed of, murdered in short, thus saving a tiring and unnecessary journey. It appeared that this gnarled-looking character was a Gallipoli veteran who had no particular liking for the British, let alone the Greeks. Fortunately for us, the officer, although he listened carefully to these pleas, took little notice of them, evidently deciding to play it by the book. As the journey proceeded my morale improved; except that I had come ashore in gym-shoes and was finding the path, such as it was, extremely uncomfortable.

Eventually we arrived in a small poverty-stricken town called Yoran. It had a dishevelled open square, at one end of which, to my great joy, were the remains of an enormous Greek marble temple. It was the temple of Apollo at Didyma, and I had been hoping against hope that this was where the Turkish HQ might be. At first no one took much notice of us, and we sat on the ground for half an hour or so watching a group of fairly primitive conscripts being instructed in how to take a German machine gun to pieces. Eventually we were interrogated at some length by the man with the white horse and a more senior officer, after which we were given a plate of soup and put to bed in the near-by police station. The night seemed long and uncomfortable, the straw pallets hard, but by divine providence there were neither bugs nor fleas. Early next morning things took a turn for the better. Instructions from on high had come through by phone, to the effect that we should be returned to our ship and told to leave Turkish waters forthwith: just what we wished to do. The atmosphere became almost friendly (despite the Gallipoli veteran, still lurking around from time to time and casting baleful glances in our direction), so I asked if I could spend half an hour wandering round the ruins. Permission was granted, and almost everyone in sight came with me.

In theory I knew quite a lot about this huge unfinished temple, of 3rd-century BC construction but containing within it an earlier shrine, rather like the great church at Assisi. My informal lecture as we clambered round was evidently much appreciated; for me, of course, it was deeply exciting to see my first major Greek antiquity, especially after very little sleep and in somewhat bizarre circumstances. All in all it was a fascinating morning, after which we walked back, in a far more relaxed state of mind than on the journey inland the previous day, down to the coast. This time I *was* offered a ride on horseback, which I accepted out of politeness until it became too uncomfortable. The crew and the rest of the Sacred Greeks were touchingly relieved to welcome us back. They thought they had seen the last of us, and were on the point of radio-ing back to base for further instructions. As it was, we sat out the rest of daylight and headed off at dusk, with feelings of rejoicing, into the wine-dark sea.

Course was set south of Gaidharo and then of the Fournoi Islands. By 2 a.m. the weather was deteriorating and we were making slow progress; by dawn I decided to close the southern shore of Ikaria (a long, steep and mountainous island) and hope for some shelter from the northerly-westerly gale. Actually the gusts from the mountains – the so-called catabatic winds – grew fiercer as we approached the coast more closely, and we were forced to take shelter right inshore, in St Nicholas bay, where a small crowd of locals gathered to greet us. I rowed ashore with a couple of boxes of food, and stayed awhile practising my Greek on an unexpected new acquaintance, a sophisticated and extremely pretty girl who was redolent neither of garlic nor of the nunnery. By dusk the weather was improving a bit and I had to cut short for ever this burgeoning friendship as we headed westward for Dragonisi, a useful little islet close up against the eastern coast of Mykonos.

146

In the event we decided to press on and land our party that night, in St Anna bay on Mykonos itself, from where we moved by dawn to Kalofata bay just to the south. At midday a Greek arrived with a note from the reconnaissance party that the Germans in Mykonos town were barricaded in and short of food; we could leave them temporarily to their own devices, taking off our own party without further ado that same evening and moving on to land them on Andros to the north. All went according to plan; we picked up our men, augmented by three civilian refugees, then cruised up through the concealing darkness past the sacred island of Delos and along the western coast of Tinos, landing our group just before dawn in Plaka bay, Andros, where we berthed alongside the rocks after establishing that there were no enemy in the immediate vicinity.

That day we made two forays out to sea to intercept and question two large passing caiques. The Germans had commandeered a certain number of local craft, but many of those chugging slowly between the islands were too slow for military work, and were innocently trying to carry on a bit of residual inter-island trade, mostly in much-needed foodstuffs. There was serious starvation in some of the islands by 1944, especially in barren places like Syros which had a relatively large population, including a German and Italian one, and little home-grown produce. Even the relatively fertile Naxos had its problems. Our two intercepts proved to be innocent, so far as we could tell, so we let them proceed on their way. By evening the weather was deteriorating – this was late August, and the difficult *meltemi* or Etesian wind was still blowing up strongly from time to time. Next day all lines were out to hold us in our half-sheltered bay.

The reconnaissance party returned that evening, but there was no possibility of leaving in that weather. They reported that local guerrillas were watching out for Germans, in case they sent patrols out from Andros town. Next day found us still weatherbound, though the wind showed signs of moderating. That was just as well, since in the late afternoon a bandolier-laden character came on board to say that the German garrison had been informed of our presence. I got the underlying message, which was that we had better leave *instanter*, and that the people who wanted us to do so were precisely the local guerrilla bunch, the ELAS gang, who did not like our interest in Andros affairs and passing shipping. That was interfering with their own steadily tightening grip on local matters in the interest of international Communism. However much the Germans knew or did not know (and it was more probable than not that ELAS had informed on us), there was little point in arguing the toss. We therefore left at once in a moderate and uncomfortable sea, to anchor for the night in Marmara cove in Tinos. This lay fairly close by and immediately to the south; reports of the German radar caique mentioned in our Sailing Orders were disappointingly found to be erroneous.

There we were weather-bound for a further day, and the same sort of guerrilla problems arose. My log records that at 1815 an armed party had to be sent to the near-by village to retrieve a Greek officer and his telegraphist, detained by Communist guerrillas from Euboea. At the same time the release of two caiques operated by ISLD (another of the various and from our point of view often superfluous British intelligence organizations) was negotiated. Once again I was quite glad to extricate us from shore-bound complications – this trip was revealing a great deal about the complexity of allied relations with Turkey on the one hand, and the increasingly more obstreperous Greek resistance groups on the other. The good old days when one could count on the support of almost any Greek islander were coming to an end, at least in the chain of islands running down from Euboea and the mainland into the central Aegean.

Our course was now eastward and homeward by way of Dragonisi (Dragon's Island) and, it was supposed, Sirina. It was in Dragonisi, incidentally, that on an earlier trip I had received concrete proof of the effectiveness of our camouflage nets, despite their inconvenience. I had been relieving myself on deck, more or less under the netting, shortly before dawn when a small Greek fishing boat approached, its skipper throwing out a grapnel from about four metres away at what he thought to be a convenient bit of rock. I saw it coming, and waited with interest. His face, as it sank silently into the netting, was a picture. I was not about to camouflage this time, in any case; but the approach to the rocky little inlet around this particular midnight looked unappealing in a roughish sea, so I decided to head for nearby Delos – not a regular port of call, but tempting in this weather, not least on a personal level for its antiquities. In the early hours we first secured alongside the mole in the tiny boat-harbour there, but were urgently asked to move by a slightly-built man who emerged from the darkness to identify himself as resident MO4 agent. He conjured up a small motor-boat which led us into a small bay some three sea-miles away, in the south of the near-by and almost deserted island of Rheneia. This place is famous for its tomb-groups, since in ancient times no one was allowed to die on Apollo's sacred island of Delos, so that the moribund (along with expectant mothers, a different source of pollution) were ferried over to Rheneia to complete the job. My new friend, who had a radio operator on Rheneia and lived in a shepherd's hut there, explained that Delos was too conspicuous for a boat even of our size, and might compromise his own operations. Incidentally he was able to give us a good deal of the kind of information we ourselves needed, at least about Delos and Rheneia itself.

The caique was safe in Rheneia for the day, and I was still determined, if possible, to view the marvellous ruins of Delos. My agent friend agreed to run me back in his motor-boat, soon after dawn, to the sacred isle. The hours that followed were breathtaking. Delos, as everyone knows, is still exciting, even with cruise-ships filling the channel between Rheneia and Delos and landing tourists by the hundreds in the tiny harbour there. It is still, in a way, solitary, since there are no hotels and everyone has to be off the island before dusk. But *then* it was still more secret and undefiled, with a certain spice added by the knowledge of enemy-occupied islands visible on every side. And it was the first really extensive site I had seen, the great sanctuary which (together with Apollo's other shrine at Delphi) dominated the imaginations of the Greeks from even before Homer. Now the guardian of the museum and his small family were its only occupants, together with a goat-herd or two in summer. It was a piercingly brilliant and wind-swept day; I was shown everything, at least in the monumental area. My agent friend was by now extremely relaxed, and we climbed together to the top of little Mount Kynthos to see the whole of the central Cyclades laid out beneath us, with Mykonos close by to the east, Tinos to the north, Syros to the west, and the great bulk of Naxos visible through slight haze southwards. Below us the ruin-strewn stony soil of Delos itself, with the rocky islets of the Rhevmatia channel and the arid fields of Rheneia, were set off against a brilliant blue streaked with white as the wind blew the tops off the serried waves of a typically short Aegean sea.

Sight-seeing on Delos; author in the centre, the agent on his left.

150

Such magical interludes do not (I was to learn once again) last for ever. Descending to the museum around lunchtime we found a messenger waiting from Rheneia, to say that something of an emergency had arisen. One of our HDML's had been caught by the Germans in Sirina, and all Aegean operations were compromised by the capture of the code-books on board. LS 12 certainly could not leave its present berth much before dark, so we waited an hour or so more (refreshing ourselves with coarse bread and a little retsina) before crossing over in the agent's motor-boat back to Rheneia.

By 5 p.m. I was back on board, and was shown the following two signals by the wireless operator:

To: All Ships Aegean   From: FOLEM
    SECRET
    Codes, code-books and caique recognition signals all
    believed compromised as result of capture of ML 1381
    by enemy.
To: Comaro I; Advanced Raiding Forces H.Q.; C.F.E.;
    C.F.B. Castelorizo; ML 1398; ML 1051; ML 1307;
    AHS 1; AHS 12; AHS 11   From: FOLEM
    IMMEDIATE
1. Must assume all current operations compromised
2. What intelligence or orders did ML 1381 carry that
    could be of value to the enemy?

Telegraphist Thornton, who was extremely competent, had already appended the following pencilled note to the last signal:
Sir:
I.   Our signal sent this morning was in '1 TIME PAD' and
    is perfectly secure. I received FOLEM's signal before
    transmitting your signal and consequently altered the
    code.
II. If AGOX is compromised *all* our signals except this
    morning's are liable to have been read by enemy.

151

III. Germans *cannot* decode our signal sent this morning.
IV. Call-signs are probably compromised, but that will not affect us immediately.

– I have passed your instructions on to Cox'n re look-out towards Syros.

Sparks

Thus it was clear that, although my last report had been sent out by one-time pad (where the code was unbreakable), earlier signals had been sent in a code that would reveal us to be in the area. This, together with probable collaboration between ELAS and the German garrison in Andros about our position and intentions, persuaded me that an early start would be in order – in other words, to get clear of the Cyclades like a bat out of hell and make best speed towards the Turkish coast. Our mission was, after all, accomplished, and we were on our way home in any case.

There was a further motive for haste. Sparks happened to have come to the end of his first one-time pad booklet, and on reaching for its sole successor from the very back of the signals locker had found it to be half devoured by our resident and ineradicable family of mice, and therefore unusable. Secure communication with base was no longer possible. With this additional motive for haste I decided to depart in full daylight, by 6 p.m., marginally supplementing our engine speed with full sail. This, I hoped, might also make us look even more like a Greek fishing-vessel than usual, for the benefit of the German look-out post some two miles away on the south coast of Mykonos. Course was set for Gaidharos far to the east of us, passing between Patmos and the Fournoi Islands, and with a stiff north-westerly and a following sea we made outstanding progress, regaining Turkish waters by breakfast-time and, after a brief stop in Pharlah bay (if only to make some single point of contact with our route according to Sailing Orders), being back at base in Deremen some twelve hours later. We were, I think, lucky to have had such a straightforward passage home. At all events, it was the end of

152

an exciting ten-day trip. Mykonos, Andros, Tinos and Delos had produced all the intelligence about the central islands that was immediately needed; Delos in addition had revealed more perennial secrets, helping to determine more surely my own activities for the future. As for Sirina and the ML, our thoughts were downcast; though Barbayiannis and his family, at least, came to no harm. That little island was almost too good to be true, and had probably been used to excess in the preceding weeks.

LS 12 was overdue for a re-fit, and there was in any case to be a slight lull in flotilla activities. At dawn on September 1st, therefore, we took sundry passengers on board and headed back for Beirut by way of Sertcheh, Castelorizo and Paphos. After a marvellous week of leave in and around Beirut (when I could, I suppose, have copied out Professor Dawkins' dirty Crusader lyrics at Krak, but had other things to do), followed by sundry frustrations in dealing with tricky Mr Hammer and his repair staff, we were back in the Aegean by the end of the month.

By now the situation had altered: Chios had been evacuated by the enemy, and John Campbell (back in place as Comaro I) had decided to move our base up there from the Gulf of Kos. LS 12 and LS 4 loaded up with soldiers and stores in Castelorizo and proceeded in company to escort the big head-quarters schooner, LS 36, up to the new centre of operations. The journey was uneventful except for a bit of the more exotic kind of Aegean weather in the early morning of October 2nd. LS 36 had been temporarily left behind; with LS 4 we were off Symi when there arose a sudden and violent electrical storm. Wind-speed increased to gale-force, the sea became confused, blackness was Stygian between brilliant sheets of lightning, during one of which not one but two considerable water-spouts were seen close on our starboard bow. By then we were hove-to and had lost contact with the other caique. Fortunately after a hectic hour or so the weather started to calm down as rapidly as it had blown up. The two boats found each other and proceeded thankfully round Cape Krio. That may be anthropomorphizing them a bit; the thought also occurred for a moment, to me at least, that the high life of Beirut had its advantages now that winter was i'cumin in. A similar storm was to strike my little yacht *Stella Falcon* (with myself, Robert Ballantine and his wife on board) some twenty years later in the Gulf of Taranto, also in October. Mrs Ballantine was unperturbed, but on the whole I prefer my small-boat sailing without water-spouts.

CHAPTER 10

The Steno Pass and Life in Chios

The nature of our operations in the Aegean was clearly chang-ing rapidly at this time. For the previous three months the emphasis had been on landing reconnaissance parties, their function to find out how tightly the islands were being held. The enemy had been gradually reducing garrisons in the smaller islands, even in their larger divisional bases in Rhodes, Leros, Samos, Syros and Melos. Now some of the lesser islands were being abandoned completely, as too prone to attack; the fact that in Mykonos, for example, the remaining garrison at the time of our recent visit was demoralized and largely confined to barracks was a case in point. Raids like that on Symi in the Dodecanese, and on a less elaborate scale Santorin in the southern Cyclades, were bad for German morale, and had hastened the day of total evacuation. That day, with the abandonment of Chios, was obviously now approaching, and our main priority was to discover when the major withdrawals from Melos, Rhodes and the other big bases were likely to take place, with the idea that some of the few destroyers, even a cruiser or two, that FOLEM was now able to send up into the Aegean could make a killing. In addition, an intensive effort was under way to put food sup-plies into the islands, like Tinos indeed, that had already been evacuated.

On the other side of the account the Germans were at last becoming more sophisticated in dealing with our small-boat operations, and about now they began to move around an élite cadre of some 300 'Brandenburger' commandos, landing them for a day or two on one or other of the smaller Dodecanese Islands – which gave rise to many reports of impending counter-attacks and threats of re-occupation. For me in LS 12, and no doubt for several other colleagues in the flotilla (whose detailed movements, because we were away from base so much and so isolated on our own particular operations, one did not often hear about until much later), the next month was to be an exceptionally crowded one, and our functions extremely diverse.

Three days after arrival in Chios I set off in LS 12 for Panormos bay in north-eastern Tinos, in company with an HDML, a biggish schooner, and four Greek food caiques. After an elaborate welcome from the locals we crossed to Mykonos to pick up a patrol that night; then back to Tinos, and across to northern Syros to land another patrol the next evening, evidently just missing an E-boat as we arrived. The reception party in Syros further reported that the enemy garrison was due to be evacuated that very same night. All these bits of news were of course passed straight back to Comaro, who pieced them together with other reports from elsewhere and recommended appropriate action to Alexandria. Meanwhile we returned to Panormos bay in Tinos, where three guerrilla caiques had the effrontery to steal our dinghy. That was dealt with and they were sent back to Euboea – for various political reasons they could not be impounded. Next day we set off westwards to Port Oryes in Keos, towing a dory which left with its reconnaissance party close to midnight; then back to Tinos where we spent a day or so ferrying around Italian prisoners. Now we could move over to Syros itself, entering the abandoned harbour on Sunday afternoon, October 15th. The next day, back to Keos, where we scurried from one bay to the next looking for our patrol. Eventually they were picked up and we returned to Syros, where life became momentarily more challenging.

As we entered harbour there a signal was received that a German destroyer with 300 troops was reported to be in

Panormos. That turned out to be not strictly accurate, but at least here was evidence of possible enemy naval movements around the north-east coast of Tinos, itself some twenty miles north of where we lay in Syros. Late that afternoon I decided that we had to move back towards Panormos, or at least as far as the Steno Pass, to see what was going on. Steno Pass (known in Greek as Dhysvaton Stenon or 'Difficult Strait') is the narrow gap, a mile and a half wide, that separates the southern tip of Andros from the northern tip of Tinos, with Panormos bay some six miles through and beyond it down to the south-east. To begin with we could sail up under the eastern coast of Syros, but then there was an open-sea crossing of some twelve miles, half of it to be done in daylight. At six and a half knots one felt horribly exposed to aerial investigation, but the Germans presumably had larger concerns at the moment than the movements of a small fishing vessel. Darkness when it came was a relief, all the same. I felt we should have left Syros earlier, but in retrospect had judged it about right.

As we approached the Steno Pass itself, by now sheltered in darkness (in fact by a moonless night that was as black as pitch), I had for the time being to concentrate on not running aground, since I wanted to keep within a hundred yards or so of the tall rocky islet, some quarter-mile long and close to the Tinos shore, on which stood a small but of course non-functioning lighthouse. Between that and the cliffs of Tinos was another and slightly larger rock, 'Monks' Island', which ran to within just over a hundred yards of the cliffs. That this little stretch of water was clear of rocks and shallows – of less than two fathoms, that is, which was all right for us – was confirmed by a useful large-scale plan on Admiralty chart no. 1630. Not that all this seemed very relevant as we drew near to the lighthouse rock on our starboard side, since I had decided by now that I had to press on closer to Panormos Bay itself. But suddenly one of the crew gave a loud whisper: 'Looks like there's some kind of ship on the port bow, skipper.' He had good eyesight; even through binoculars little could be seen about what kind of craft it was: a mere slowly moving shadow. Could be an E-boat? No larger, at any rate, and puzzling in its movements, for it seemed to be turning down towards Monks' Island. I came hard-a-starboard to seek the shadows of the tiny gap between the lighthouse islet and Monks' Island. We could by now hear the faint sound of a motor; it was not a chug-chug or single-stroke diesel, which most Greek caiques had, but otherwise we were little the wiser.

There now began a curious fandango in which both craft slipped twice around the lighthouse rock, and in my case once through the shallow passage between Monks' Island and the Tinos shore, each trying to remain hidden at the same time as getting a glimpse of what the opposition might be. It was, as I mentioned before, a very dark night, fortunately with little sea. Certainly there was not much speed available on either side, and fears about an E-boat receded. At last I got a good look; the other boat was after all, chug-chug or not, a caique very like ourselves. Could it be damnable MO4 again? I rather thought this was not their scene; yet a German craft was improbable – a Greek one, at this time of night, little less so.

Yet this ritual game of hide-and-seek was wasting time and had to stop. Proceeding towards Panormos was not necessarily a good idea, and these people, whoever they were, might know something that I did not know. So, after making doubly sure that our little bits of armament were ready for action, I suddenly turned back out of the deepest shadows of the lighthouse channel and got within hailing distance. '*Poios eisthe?*', 'Who are you?' seemed a reasonable approach. '*Psarades, psarades*' ('fishermen, fishermen') came the reply, followed by 'And who are *you*?' – 'We're English Navy' – 'Welcome, then!' It all seemed above-board and I drew closer, at least to within better shouting-distance. I instantly went on to ask about the German craft in Panormos, to be told No, there wasn't one, but that a German *battleship* had passed by about half an hour ago, close to the eastern end of Steno Pass and heading northwards at about ten knots. Sparks encoded a brief enemy report to this effect, and it was despatched within three minutes. I did not have time for subtleties about whether it was a battleship or not – certainly not, since the Germans did not have any in the Aegean and if so it would not be sauntering around at slow speed. Interpretation would be done by John Campbell, who knew far better than I that all largeish naval craft were 'battleships' in the eyes of Greek fishermen (just as, by a curious and contrary rhetorical figure, a genuine British battleship, the *King George V*, was once described to me as 'the big English caique').

Having ascertained that the German ship, whatever it was, had passed out of our ken, that Panormos was empty, and that our enemy report was safely transmitted, there was little to do except wish good-night to our still rather mysterious Greek friends and turn back to Syros, where we retired thankfully to our bunks just before dawn. I did not have time to quiz those Greeks about what they were doing there in the middle of the night – certainly not fishing; that remained a puzzle. Yet the encounter was fruitful in martial terms, since the enemy report, duly interpreted, led to the interception and sinking, some four hours later, by one of our light cruisers, of a large German sea-going transport barge carrying some 250 troops being evacuated from Melos (I think) up to Salonica. Fifty years on one wishes they had reached Salonica safe and sound, but then things seemed different.

A couple of days later ML 354 arrived in Syros to relieve me; that evening we loaded five German prisoners on board and headed back toward Chios. I wrote an account of those prisoners a year or two later, for my own purposes, and give the gist of it here. As usual the weather was none too good and rapidly became worse. As we emerged from the Steno Pass around midnight the wind was south-easterly force 7, sea moderate to rough. There was a longish open-sea crossing to Chios, so I decided to seek temporary shelter in Korthi bay, Andros, not least because the German passengers were adding to the discomfort of life on board. As the caique lurched sickeningly from side to side, with the wind howling through the rigging and heavy spray tearing over the canvas side-screens, they huddled grimly on the big hatch-cover on deck, burying themselves under a tarpaulin. Ahead, through the spray and the darkness, I could see the dim outline of the hills above Korthi. It could only be four or five miles off. I leant on the tiller to alter course for where the bay should be. As the sea came on the beam the rolling became heavier, gunwale under every time. Conditions were nearly dangerous, not quite. The prisoners evidently thought otherwise, since one of them extricated himself from the tarpaulin and crawled down the deck towards me. I recognized the blonde one who spoke English, and told him to get back amidships. Instead of obeying, he collapsed on the deck and clawed at my legs in supplication. He sobbed and implored me to save him and his companions, accusing me *en passant* of ill-treatment and breaking international law. They had no lifebelts, he said. He was a bedraggled, pathetic object, evidently no seaman. I mentioned to him that if he continued to disobey orders I should be forced to lock him up down below, where conditions were much worse. Furthermore, there *were* no lifebelts. If he kept his friends quiet the passengers would share no worse a fate than the crew. Soon I called over to the Coxswain to take the tiller, and made my way to the waist of the boat where the prisoners were lying. They had spewed all over the place and were wet and frightened; I told them through the blonde one that with luck we should find shelter in an hour or so. Feeling slightly queasy myself, I returned aft. The coast was drawing closer and we were getting some shelter from the north, but there was still no sign of the expected bay.

Eventually we found it, and motored cautiously in toward the shore, sounding with the lead as we edged closer to a small jetty. At three fathoms we dropped anchor, only to haul it up again as the boat dragged fast at the first heavy gust from the hills. Three times more we re-layed it before finding tolerable holding-ground. Then a guard was set over the prisoners and the rest of us dried off and went to sleep. When dawn came I clambered out on deck and saw that we were lying about two hundred yards from the shore, around which clustered a score of low white cottages. A small fishing boat was pushing off from the beach to have a closer look at us. As it approached I leant over the side and shouted good morning to its four suspicious Greek occupants. At this they nosed closer, and one of them stood up in the boat to see what our caique – which was flying a Greek flag with the German red-and-white permit pennant beneath it – was carrying on deck. One of the first things he saw was the heap of sodden field-grey uniforms that concealed the prisoners, and above them, seated on the main hatch, a seaman with a tommy-gun. The islander looked relieved, and behind his heavy beard appeared to smile.

'Germans?' he asked; 'then you must be English: *prepei na eisthe Ingzlezoi*.' 'English, English,' the other three shouted, and climbed over the canvas side-screen to shake me warmly by the hand. Three of the crew had appeared from below to see what the commotion was, and they too were affectionately greeted. Fortunately the man with the gun was left with an unimpeded view of his charges, not that they had much spirit for deeds of resistance. Tea was on the boil and I offered our new Greek friends a mug each, which they received with delight, tea being almost unknown in those years of dearth. I enquired what the situation on the island was. Bad, very bad, they replied. The Germans had all left, they had been sunk at sea it was to be hoped, but in their place were the communist guerrillas: false Greeks, they said. Ah, Captain, they said, they terrorize our lives. The Germans had been worse, yes; they were fiends in disguise. Couldn't I see that from the degenerate faces of the prisoners there? (Actually they had recovered a bit from their craven stupor, but looked unhappy again, and a bit fearful, when they saw the Greeks on board.) I had no special desire to discuss the prisoners, and turned to the question of the best place to moor up. They indicated a small buoy that was strong enough to hold us, and would enable us to secure the stern to the end of the ruined jetty. So we set about shifting the caique to the new berth; then the other occupants of the houses, mostly women, came down to the water's edge to stare at the strange and evidently benevolent Englishmen.

It was not long before they, too, spotted the prisoners. At this moment the cook was just dishing out breakfast, and I noticed without too much surprise that the prisoners' ration was the same as our own. 'Coxswain,' I said sternly, 'don't you remember my saying yesterday that while these men are on board they're to be treated as prisoners, not as pet rabbits? That means they have to be given enough plain food to keep them healthy, and no more. You'd be surprised how little that is according to international law. Now they're lapping up the last of the fresh tomatoes. If you must waste fresh food, I'd rather it was thrown overboard, or given, rather, to these half-starved bloody Greeks.'

Leading Seaman King, normally no softy, certainly no enemy-lover, leant against the tiller and looked aggrieved. 'Look, Sir,' he replied, 'if this were a big ship it would be different. Then the prisoners would be down below and they'd have their food by themselves, and I should be happy enough to know that they were on a diet of bread and water for a change. But, as it is, they have to be up on deck within five yards of where we're having our own dinner; and we couldn't enjoy our food, after what you will agree was a sticky old night, if they were sitting there gazing at us with their eyes popping out. On a boat like this everyone on board has to have the same.'

'Personally speaking I agree with you. They're a depressing enough bunch already, and would be worse on empty bellies. It would put me off my food just as much as you; I'm not really so tough, it's just that I think one ought to try to be! But the real point is now, in any case, that all these half-starved Greeks are watching. None of them has eaten as much food as this for three years, and it's hardly fair to expect them to understand our arguments about cramped conditions on board. As long as we're here, the prisoners will have to feed on the kind of stuff the Greeks have to live on.' 'Aye aye, Sir,' the

Coxswain replied; 'but I'll just go and chase those bloody Greeko's away so that we can get down to our grub in peace.'

Unfortunately the damage had been done, and a storm of resentment against the prisoners aroused. They had already started their food. Squatting on deck, they shovelled it down as though they had not eaten for a week. With every mouthful their gloom lifted and they regained something of the status of human beings, their apathy and apparent degeneracy dropping away from them. It was something of a relief, really – to the rest of us on board, but not to the tragic chorus of black-clad Greek matrons who, despite the Coxswain's best efforts, still peered angrily over the stern. They were standing on tiptoe, craning their necks, leaning this way and that, to see what food the prisoners were eating now. One of them managed to climb onto the gunwale for a moment to get a better view, jumping down again with a cry in which delight and horror were mixed – delight at the appearance of the food, horror that these hated men were allowed to eat it. A buzz of excitement rose from the group as they realized what the prisoners were having; scattered phrases reached me, 'potatoes', 'tea with milk in it', 'meat, meat'. They were completely silent for a minute or so, and then, after some urgent whispering between themselves, one of them – the oldest judging by her withered face and prominent moustache – climbed on board and walked along the deck to where I was sitting. Like all her race, she was a democrat, and under the impetus of righteous indignation the scrupulous respect she would normally have had for my calling and nationality totally disappeared.

'Look here, young Sir,' she said, 'why in the name of the all-holy Virgin are you feeding these pigs as though they were kings? If you have food to waste, then give it to us, whose children are growing up deformed because they're starving. If you had lived on this island, and seen the way these swine behave, you wouldn't be giving them your tit-bits. Hand the pigs over to us, that's what you should do, and we'll tear their finger-nails out one by one before we kill them.' The gesture that accompanied this threat was blood-curdling in the extreme, and the other women joined in with fierce movements and raised voices. That *they* knew how to treat prisoners was the gist of their response.

I decided to deal with the matter once and for all. 'All right,' I replied; '*you* can have the prisoners, and do to them exactly what you want.' The result was inevitable: they looked sheepish and confused, muttered together for a bit and then slowly withdrew along the little jetty and onto the beach. The prisoners themselves, fortunately for them, did not follow this particular exchange, and started trying to dry out their saturated clothing. We were stuck in that bay for another thirty-six hours, during which international tensions gradually relaxed.

At last we were back in Chios, which presented a startling new appearance with cruisers and a small aircraft-carrier lying offshore. Any illusion that we should be having a day or two of rest was dispelled next morning, when we were sent off to Patmos in place of LS 5, which had broken down. The next ten days were active enough, but lacked a central theme as we scurried round from Patmos to the surrounding small islands (Arki, Lipso, Pharmako), which were full of rumours of impending German attack, presumably from the famous 300 Brandenburgers. Small patrols were landed, together with food, and taken off again. A radio link was re-established in Levitha. The most exciting thing we did was to tow out a Sacred Greek dory to just off Leros (still heavily occupied), where they landed a couple of observers ashore: not a job I should have liked. Three nights later there was panic as the observers, or non-observers rather, who had been holed up in a cellar from almost the moment of landing, urgently demanded to be taken off. As we passed through the Lipso channel, dory in tow, two British MTBs roared past, and were still optimistically putting up Oerlikon tracer an hour later. Eventually I contacted them by W/T and arranged that they should lie stopped a mile or so to the south and be prepared to create a further diversion in case the dory was spotted on its return. Meanwhile we had despatched the Greek pick-up party from a couple of miles off the Leros coast. This time I envied them still less, because an almost full moon had risen and the surface of the sea was gleaming like gold. As the Greeks clambered down into the dory they called out patriotic slogans, 'Liberty or death' and the like; that was the Mediterranean way, but these were brave men. Fortunately they returned safely a couple of hours later with their two bedraggled comrades from the cellar.

By breakfast time we were back in Port Grico, Patmos; next morning it was off again with a small raiding-force patrol to have a look at the Fournoi Islands, close to Samos. It was considered safe enough nowadays to make the two-and-a-half hour crossing in daylight. Once secured along the rocks in a shallow indentation of the main island our soldiers headed for the village, while I climbed the near-by hill for exercise and the view. After twenty minutes two stalwart Greek village women appeared and joined me as I reclined at leisure on the grass. After a few casual sentences one of them said how brave we English were. I tried to look modest and replied that it was nothing, really. The Germans were on the run and would cause little more trouble. 'Yes, but even so, Capetanios, it is still brave of you to be taking your leisure up here in the afternoon sun when there are three hundred Germans just down in the village, only twenty minutes' walk away.'

I would like to think that at this moment I preserved my *sang froid*; in fact I sprang to my feet like a scalded cat and indulged in a few urgent 'what?' and 'where?' questions. At last, it appeared, we had managed to coincide with the almost mythical Brandenburgers, whose existence I had been beginning to doubt. I bid a hasty farewell, saying that urgent duties called me, and sped back down the hill. The patrol was speeding back equally urgently from the direction of the village, where they had gathered the same information. At least they had picked up a suspected quisling on the way. Within minutes we were back on board, pushing away from the rocks and finally heading southward in the late afternoon

165

sunlight. There was a certain nervousness in the air, but the Brandenburgers had evidently been so busy terrifying the locals that they had not noticed the gallant visitors from a neighbouring island.

After a couple more days in Patmos, AHS 22 – one of the Greek flotilla – arrived to take over. We sailed for Chios with the dory in tow, pausing for shelter in the south-west corner of Samos. It was early November by now and the weather was erratic. Two events during the week that followed are hard to forget. The first was relatively light-hearted, being the celebration of Guy Fawkes day, Chios-style. As darkness fell two of the off-lying destroyers decided to loose off some star-shell over the town. That got them into trouble later, but meanwhile it persuaded the Greek troops ashore that this strange British celebration was indeed to be taken seriously. They therefore roamed the quayside spraying tracer bullets into the air; everyone became very excited and a good deal of drinking was done. Miraculously there were no casualties, even when later that night one of the Sacred Greeks expended his last magazine into the roof of the long dormitory where some of our own men were quartered.

The second event was less public but more serious. I received an urgent message to present myself at once before the then acting Comaro-figure (not John Campbell) and the Brigadier in command of British troops ashore. I searched my conscience but could detect no misdeed deserving of reprimand from such a distinguished inter-service duo. It was gradually revealed to me, after a good deal of coughing and spluttering from these two senior officers, what this was about. It should be explained that a good deal of trouble in Chios was being caused by a Greek called Petrides, head of the local branch of EAM, the political wing of the Communist guerrilla movement. Mr P. was quite a fiery orator – I had heard him in action a few nights before – and was having some slight success in stirring up the generally quiescent Chiotes into irritating though not immediately dangerous forms of political malaise.

Evidently the military authorities had become concerned, and decided that the simplest thing was for Petrides to be put out of action. EAM was not at this time an illegal organisation, therefore he could not simply be arrested. What these two great minds before me had decided, therefore, was that he should be simply *got rid of* – not abducted and removed elsewhere, for example, which would have been just tolerable though probably unwise, but, as they say, positively bumped off. All this was hesitantly and circuitously explained to me – who could, needless to say, scarcely believe what I was hearing. Then came the final piece of subtlety and refinement. The person who was to do the bumping-off, of course (though this was put in more euphemistic terms), was evidently my good self; the reason for my selection, that I spoke by this time quite tolerable Greek. What was to happen, according to this brilliant plan, was that I was to invite Petrides one fine afternoon – as soon as possible, in fact – to come for a pleasure excursion in my caique, in the waters between Chios and the closely facing Turkish coast. When I returned, he would no longer be on board. There was no mention of tying weights to him or encasing him in cement; obviously the best thing was to keep it simple, just a quick nudge overboard as one pointed out the beauties of the seascape or handed him a welcoming glass of retsina. My crew, of course, were to be enthusiastic sharers in the conspiracy.

The absurdity and folly, as well as the sheer wickedness, of this whole rigmarole is almost unbelievable, especially coming from a couple of experienced officers who in other respects were regarded as quite good at their jobs. The Brigadier, indeed, was much loved among his troops, or so it was said. My own demeanour during the interview, which lasted for something over half an hour, was fairly calm; I managed to interpose a number of questions, designed I suppose to make clearer the total unsuitability of what was being suggested. Did they, for example, really think that Petrides would accept such an invitation, and not immediately suspect a plot? And would he not be missed, after waving good-bye to his Communist friends on the quayside and sailing off for this pleasant maritime tea-party? And would not Sub-Lieutenant Kirk, RNVR, be somehow associated with his going missing? Also, might not the disappearance of Mr P. make him a martyr, causing someone equally odious to be promoted in his place?

These were some of the preliminary points to be raised; the larger ethical question was one that I felt could be reserved for the time being. But before that, and after ten more minutes of such logical games and consequent prevarications, I at last had the sense to ask the key question. It was very simple, and was addressed to the Lieutenant-Commander (to whom, after all, and not to some bumbling Brigadier, my technical allegiance lay): 'Sir, may I request these orders in writing?'

There was a long silence. Both my interlocutors looked shifty and embarrassed, or even more so than they were already. They conferred briefly in lowered voices, and then the Brigadier uttered as follows: 'Look, Kirk, I think we'd better drop the whole thing, for the time being at least. And kindly keep it to yourself.' 'Aye aye Sir,' I replied, and left the room. The rest of the day was spent in a state of continuing disbelief at the shortcomings, and occasional sheer malignity, of the military mind.

Chios in any case was a bit of a hole; the final straw was the enforced brothel-inspection organized (as described earlier) by the rejuvenated Ron Taylor. On November 13th I left on a trip that was like a breath of fresh air. It was to last for three full weeks down to the southern Dodecanese, to Symi again, in company with a dashing and truly delightful companion, Captain Dick Harden, SBS, accompanied by four Other Ranks.

CHAPTER 11

A Trip with Captain Harden, SBS

The gist of my Sailing Orders for this escape from bureaucracy and attempted murder in Chios (a strong claimant, incidentally, to be Homer's birthplace) was as follows:

(1) Having embarked five all ranks, wireless set and stores proceed at 1600, 12th November, to Symi via Turkish territorial waters.

(2) You will cooperate with Captain Harden in carrying out recces on Piscopi and Nisiro. In addition you will act as W/T link at Symi.

The situation is developed a little in the corresponding Army orders, of which I received a copy:

(a) Symi is not occupied by enemy forces.

(b) BMA relief is being supplied, and Capt MacPherson, BMA, is already on the island.

(c) Nisiro is believed ungarrisoned, although reports of enemy intention to reoccupy the island have been received.

(d) Piscopi has a permanent garrison of 150 Germans which may have been reinforced recently by approx 70 all ranks from Cos.

(e) Calchi is believed ungarrisoned and Alinnia lightly held.

To this was appended a list of Intentions and Tasks:

(a) 'Establish secret W/T sta Symi.'
(b) 'Recce islands of Piscopi and Nisiro' and so on, with a good deal of repetition; the important thing, somewhat disguised in peculiar Army language, being that 'Recce patrols will be mounted at discretion of force comd and Capt of LS 12 to fulfil tasks.'

In short, we were to buzz down the coast from Chios to Symi (familiar already because of the big raid there four months earlier), set up a radio station, and have a good look round. Captain Harden had only four soldiers with him, so life on board should not be too uncomfortable. It seemed like a pleasant outing, provided that this same Harden was reasonably easy to get on with, as nearly all SBS officers were. Indeed, as soon as I set eyes on him, I recognized him as an old friend from Radlett days when we were both about ten. His family lived in a big house near the Warren, where we stalked rabbits together from time to time. In those days Dick had a slight stammer and a faintly nervous manner; the stammer remained but the apparently reserved little boy had turned into an extroverted, highly amusing and rather swashbuckling figure. We got on well and I was devastated when he was killed in action in Italy during the last months of the war there.

His sensible and relaxed qualities showed themselves about four hours after our departure from Chios. Toward midnight we were making painfully slow progress into a head sea amid spectacular lightning storms. Dick put his head up from the cabin and said, 'It's bloody uncomfortable, isn't it, Geoff? I'm even beginning to feel sea-sick – bad for us pongos, you know. W-why don't we go back to Chios and let things s-settle down a bit?' '*What* a sensible chap,' I thought, easing the tiller round till we were on the reverse course. After a few hours' shelter in southern Chios things improved somewhat, though we only made 5 knots and by teatime were sheltering in Karlovasi on the north coast of Samos. Next day we passed through the Samos strait, interrogating a Turkish coaster *en*

170

route, and put into Gumusluk for the night, where we were told that the peripatetic 300 Brandenburgers were now occupying the tiny island of Lipsos not far offshore – much good might it do them, if true.

Another day's passage followed, across the mouths of the gulfs of Mandeliyah and Kos and round Cape Krio. Soon after dawn on the 16th we entered Symi harbour to secure alongside Government House there. My log recorded the following: 'Contacted BMA representative Captain McPherson, found to be panic-stricken.' I remember the meeting well: the Captain had been made nervous by the persistent reports that the Germans from Rhodes were about to re-occupy Symi – or perhaps it was next stop for the Brandenburgers? Anyway, the Captain (who after all had come to organize the distribution of aid to the island and not to stop an invasion single-handed) was sweating and shaking heavily, and for some reason seemed inclined to put the blame on us. Dick and I assured him that he was now safe, which, considering our whole relieving force numbered fewer than a dozen, some of them admittedly fairly tough characters, seemed to calm him down to an almost unbelievable extent.

Fortunately he was sleeping it off when a Feisler Storch reconnaissance plane spent twenty minutes over the island that afternoon. That, and a further message over the radio talking about imminent attack, caused us to move the caique out of the main harbour and into a less conspicuous position in the caique-building yard, in a tiny bay just round the corner. It was so sheltered that LS 12 could be moored with its bow almost on the beach, the hope being that it would merge in with one or two half-built built caiques ashore. Unfortunately, on the very next day, three quarters of Dick's desert-trained troops managed to blow themselves up by carelessly throwing petrol onto a still burning can of sand, over which they were brewing mugs of tea. They did not die, but they burnt their hands and their feet and were definitely out of action. I managed to dissuade Captain McPherson from visiting me at the caique-yard, which now looked more like a first-aid post

171

than a centre of defensive warfare. Dick, meanwhile, remained relatively unperturbed (more so, I must say, than I did), and we planned to make a visit to Nisyros that night.

As a preliminary we sailed over to Cape Krio, the great promontory at the south-westerly extremity of Turkey, one of the haunts – like Paphos – of the goddess Aphrodite. It was no doubt some harsher Anatolian prototype that was first worshipped there; the high promontory fell unerotically to the sea on three sides in great cliffs, more suitable as a haunt of Ares or Poseidon, and it was only when the Greek settlement of Knidos was forced to move there, after the time of Alexander the Great, that the voluptuous Greek goddess became properly installed, one of her statues to be excavated years later by the divinely-named Professor Iris Love of New York University.

Our purpose was not so much to view the Hellenistic antiquities (though one could hardly help stumbling over inscribed marble blocks and architectural fragments among the tangle of shrubs near the shore) as to consult a kind of local oracle, the Allied agent who lived in one part of the lighthouse buildings on top of the cliff. I have forgotten whether he had been apprised of our visit, or whether he just climbed down out of curiosity to see who we were. At any rate it was he, and not the German agent who lived in the other part of the lighthouse, that descended. They were said to make quite a friendly team, and I and other caique and ML skippers had noticed, when sailing round the Cape in daylight as we occasionally did, that a distant figure would tend to emerge to peer down at us through binoculars, sometimes to disappear indoors and be replaced shortly by a different figure: 'It's one of yours, Heinrich.' Be that as it may, our agent, an inconspicuous man of indeterminate nationality, had no recent news about enemy troop-movements in Nisyros, which, though clearly visible on the horizon with its neat volcanic cone, lay altogether beyond his ken in intelligence terms.

We immediately returned on board, weighed anchor and set off to find out for ourselves. By half past eight that evening

172

we arrived at (or, as I added in the log, 'nearly on') the landing beach near the north-east corner of the island; the reconnaissance party went ashore in the dinghy to find that there was no easy way up the high cliffs, so we shunted them a mile or so further north where they disappeared satisfactorily into the gloom. By midnight the weather had deteriorated, so I upped anchor and chugged around just offshore; soon the party re-appeared and we headed back for the anchorage at Cape Krio, secure now in the knowledge that, despite all rumours to the contrary, Nisyros was now clear of German or Italian troops. By 2.30 a.m. I had entered Krio, not without difficulty, and was lying to a couple of anchors. After breakfast the Coxswain and one of the crew rowed ashore with a pair of gold sovereigns to improve our food supply, returning after an hour with thirteen hens and a sheep. It took three gale-swept hours to regain Symi – I had no intention of lying weatherbound at Krio much longer with that sheep lurching

Bringing the sheep on board at Cape Krio.

173

round the deck and relieving itself copiously from time to time.

Thoughts of afternoon tea and a nice rest were immediately dispelled by the news that four German soldiers had taken residence on Marmara Island, no more than a rock really, just off the north coast of Symi. Apparently they had been dropped over there from Rhodes, some days back, to find out what was going on in Symi itself. After sitting and freezing for useless nights on end they had that morning asked a Greek fisherman for news; he had, of course, immediately returned to the main harbour to report their unwanted act of colonization.

During our absence at Krio and Nisyros an HDML had turned up, no. 1352; so Dick and I decided, with its skipper, that we should proceed on that powerful craft and put paid to this zany piece of effrontery. Without having time to inform either Captain MacPherson or the island potentates (the latter, it transpired, was a mistake) we motored off in rough seas to a point about 600 yards short of the little islet. This would, it was thought, make a good target for the Bofors gun on the foredeck and thereby terrify the enemy into surrender. Dick and I made ready to go ashore – I was quite inseparable by now from my old playmate – while the bombardment took place. It was, I must confess, a bit of a fiasco. Many rounds were fired, the range being slowly decreased, without a single hit being scored. The Captain of the ML became justifiably furious, the gunners were surly and said it was too rough, but in the end the enemy ashore, hearing no doubt a lot of banging and deducing that it was meant to be directed at them, started waving their shirts from behind a substantial rock outcrop.

Eventually a couple of figures appeared with their hands up. Dick and I were rowed ashore, he with a Tommy gun and I with a Navy-issue revolver. Looking incredibly ferocious we approached the outcrop at a slow canter, when four excessively bedraggled German soldiers appeared, making every sign of wishing to surrender. What happened next was rather shocking to a simple young Sub-Lieutenant, since Dick with great speed and efficiency removed the wallets, wrist-watches and binoculars of three of them; the fourth was prudently bare of all personal wealth. The SBS were not too fussy about loot; indeed it was rumoured that on one occasion they had come across a caique-load of personal wireless-sets for German troops, and aborted their main operation for a week to sail it down to Haifa, where there was a profitable market in such things. Be that as it may, back off Symi fierce questioning about transmitters and code-books elicited the convincing answer that all that sort of thing had been thrown into the sea. So the prisoners were ferried out to the ML, and by soon after nighfall we were all back in Symi harbour. It had not, perhaps, been a very glorious afternoon (though I had a neat little Beretta automatic and some battered Zeiss binoculars as a memento), even if a vivid indication of enemy intelligence in its lowest form. But in our absence there had been some sort of panic in Symi, the rumours about invasion from Rhodes had become just too much, and several hundreds (it was claimed) of the populace had been ferried over in caiques to the Turkish coast opposite – a foolhardy enterprise with consequences (two deaths, one rape) that might have been foreseen.

Next day began a series of trips to various harbours along the facing Turkish coast that arose out of the devious mind and curious personal contacts of a Jewish sergeant, attached to Captain MacPherson, who had now taken up semi-permanent residence in the caique-yard. The idea was to intercept, or interdict, stores that were being traded between the German garrison in Rhodes and the Turks around Marmarice on the facing coast. Over the years some of the details of the personnel involved have become dim or confused. On Sunday November 19th, for example, I proceeded to Loryma to see Leonidas, another of our local agents; thence to Marmarice – in those days quite a small town – with a boat called Isabella in tow. The object was to intercept Iakovides's caique from Rhodes, a big affair that was rumoured to be stuffed with personal radio sets that the German troops there were anxious

175

to flog on the black market. That evening the weather turned bad and we had to shelter, first in Chiflik bay some miles out, then in Marmarice harbour itself. There a suitably villainous-looking messenger rowed out to say that Iakovides had successfully bribed the Kaymakam (the local civilian governor), with the consequence that his caique had managed to slip away in the night back to Rhodes. It was all rather nebulous and in the end largely unproductive, except that the Germans may have got the impression that the British were making trouble for them in Turkey, thus diverting attention from Symi. I was tired in any case of hanging around in wind-swept Turkish bays, and returned to Symi to find with interest and surprise that a small British destroyer, the Musketeer, had just arrived. The next day she was replaced by HMS Marne, and as senior British naval officer in Symi (I wondered for a moment whether some suitable acronym could be found, a forerunner perhaps of the LOLO persona that was later to bring me grief . . .) I was summoned, together with Dick, aboard.

The suggestion was that a joint reconnaissance party be landed on the neighbouring Dodecanesian island of Piscopi with a view to harassment from seaward of the enemy garrison there – mainly to encourage the Germans in Rhodes to hasten their own preparations for clearing out of the Aegean and going (or trying to go) home. So at ten that night I embarked Dick and his one still mobile soldier, together with two fleet spotting officers, and dropped them off around midnight for a good look round Piscopi. Twenty-four hours later I picked them up and returned to Symi, where two days of rough weather intervened. Then we proceeded at last to join in a shoot-up of Piscopi, together with Musketeer, another destroyer (Kelvin) which had turned up in the interval, a couple of MTBs and ML 1373. Our own part in terms of fire-power was necessarily restricted, but we were determined to use all of it. We also had a little 2" mortar on board, and after seeing three suspicious figures lurking behind some rocks on the seashore we closed the beach (it was ten o'clock of a fine

176

morning) and landed a few small mortar shells around them. Eventually a rather tense-looking figure emerged, obviously a goatherd or fisherman, and shook his fist at us; we felt ashamed and proceeded on our way. Soon we saw some genuine German soldiers up on a cliff and fired our machine-guns at them, with unknown results. Meanwhile more serious explosions had been heard from round the coast, and presumably a certain amount of confusion had been caused. At any rate they were very pleased with things back on Musketeer and down in Alex, and glowing messages were sent about gallant little caiques and so on.

It had been an interesting minor excursion, but now the Jewish sergeant and his friends had dug up more information from Marmarice; this time it was a German coaster, the 'Anna', which was due to leave there on the very next day. LS 12 dashed over there, to learn from Photis – another mysterious figure, one of the chain of half-agents, half-blackmarketeers who were playing off the British against the Turks against the Germans during those weeks and along that bit of coast – that the 'Anna's' departure had been indefinitely delayed by the Turkish harbour authorities, and that the situation was too complex, involved too much money, even for Photis to deal with. I therefore towed him back in his little caique, and decided with Dick that evening that our duties and pleasures round Symi could now be brought to a close. Rumours of German attack had declined, the W/T link ashore had been set up, Captain MacPherson was feeling better, and the three damaged soldiers needed patching up more efficiently back at base. We therefore set off at dawn on December 2nd and, after a couple of overnight stops in empty Turkish bays *en route*, arrived back in Chios just after my twenty-third birthday, after an absence of just three weeks. The war in the Aegean was running down, and this was my last fully warlike trip – a mild one of its kind though by no means without interest.

CHAPTER 12

The War is Ending; Life as LOLO

By about mid-December 1944 Athens itself had already been liberated for more than a month, the job being completed, in theory at least, by the socially-inclined Force 133 under General Scobie. The business of clearing up the Aegean islands, from which the enemy had been slower to retreat, was nearing completion. The rest of the flotilla had just been disbanded, Comaro I having recommended that most of the caiques were no longer needed and should be handed back to their original Greek owners, mainly in Samos and Symi. It was also suggested that most of us skippers, at least, were ready to volunteer for some similar job in the Far East. That was not needed in the event, and in any case my own boat (with one other Greek-manned caique) was, as it happened, to be kept operational, probably because of its recent re-fit. Therefore after three days back in Chios AHS 12 was despatched on a truly pacific mission: a seemingly gorgeous trip to report in detail on the condition of the long-disused lights and lighthouses of the central Aegean.

Basil Calamatousis, a Captain in the Welch Regiment who had found his way to Chios in some kind of liaison role and had been friendly and mildly useful there (whence his family, settled a generation since in Barry Dock in South Wales, had hailed), asked if he could come along. I was not too keen, if only because the tiny cabin was cramped even for one; but Basil suggested that his Greek friends in various islands we were to visit would undoubtedly show us a good time. His

178

superiors seemed favourable to the idea, so I agreed.

The consequences were unexpected, distinctly tragi-comical in tone. The first sign of trouble came as we entered Syros in the heart of the Cyclades. Even before we secured alongside, Basil was loudly enquiring from a considerable crowd ashore where his close friend was to be found, he being a prominent citizen of the island (which because of its 19th-century history as a coaling station contained the largest and most sophisticated town of the central Aegean). There was a marked silence from the people on the dockside, till one of them took courage to shout back *'einai sto lazareto'*, 'he's in the Lazareto'. After a moment for reflection Basil enquired about his second most important friend. I should perhaps stress that these friends had been represented to me as certain to throw tremendous parties on our behalf. The reply from ashore was similar to the first, the tone of delivery perhaps a shade more acerbic: *'kai autos sto lazareto, paidhi mou . . .'*, 'he too is in the Lazareto, mate'. As ropes were thrown ashore for securing us to the quayside I took time to ask Basil whether the Lazareto was some especially exotic hotel . . . though I knew it to be a tiny island in the harbour mouth, where a decaying building from the Turkish era, Frankish no doubt in origin, had indeed at one time housed the island's crop of lepers. Basil mumbled something about scandalous miscarriages of justice; meanwhile I had checked with one or two characters on the quayside and found that the Lazareto had been used, since the enemy had flown, for the safer incarceration of the island's most flagrant collaborators. Basil's old and influential cronies appeared to be numbers one and two on that list.

I took the liberty of mentioning to my companion, later that evening, a hope that his pre-war chums would not be causing comparable embarrassment on later stages of our trip; and suggesting that he might perhaps maintain a fairly low profile from then on. He appeared to accede. As it happens, no special friends of Basil were needed to make our two or three days stay in the town of Syros itself an outstanding

179

occasion. There were quite a few British Army people ashore, their officers a distinctly social bunch, as indeed – it appeared – were the richer Greek families in town. Elaborate parties seemed to be held almost nightly in one or other of the big 19th-century houses surrounding the quite imposing central square.

One of these parties took on a rather unusual character, when at an advanced stage of the festivities all otherwise unoccupied menfolk were quietly summoned upstairs, from the dancing that was still going on below, to our host's bedroom. There, his wife was in bed with a rather dashing character called Major Pope (I have altered his name a little). It appeared that the Major had been committing fornication in a fairly continuous way, and was just about to do so again for the fifth time. This had struck those lurking around upstairs as something of a record, given the time available and the relative seniority of the male partner; hence the summoning of a larger number of witnesses. Standing at the back of the capacious bedroom, manifestly in some kind of flurry, was a rather small man who called from time to time (perhaps too feebly in the circumstances) on the gallant Major to desist, declaring the whole business to be not *comme il faut* – the Athenian habit of speaking French in higher social circles being sometimes emulated in this small island society. He was identified for me as my host, the lady's husband. Perhaps it was under the deleterious influence of Basil (who had of course not been invited) that I was less shocked than I should have been at a scene that belonged to the pages of an Evelyn Waugh novel rather than to the generally rather starchy moral climate of the island bourgeoisie. Even so, I was respectable enough to make my way downstairs again before the fifth consummation had actually been achieved, though some ragged applause as I descended may have suggested something of the kind to be in progress.

The party I attended the following evening was, I am pleased to say, more tasteful. Perhaps even Major Pope was finding it necessary to recuperate his powers. Thereafter I was not unwilling to proceed on my legitimate business to other and less sophisticated islands, where the British Army had not yet arrived in force to alleviate the tedium of occupation. Basil, however, continued to be full of surprises, suggesting to me one quiet afternoon on passage that we should join together in purchasing a small Greek merchant ship. It was only, it seemed, of a couple of thousand tons, and fairly ancient; such things, according to my companion, were available dirt cheap at this particular moment, if one knew the right people. I evidently didn't take this suggestion seriously enough, since Basil was forced to strengthen his case by explaining that he also knew a Capetanios who would be absolutely ideal for the job. The job? At last it occurred to me, belatedly perhaps, that Basil had in mind the old Greek national custom of ship-scuttling, followed by a hefty insurance claim. That may or may not have been a false interpretation, but it temporarily aroused, once again, my youthful indignation. I therefore suggested that Basil might be suffering from too much sun and wind and should retire to rest, which he did, leaving me to reflect on the corrupt ambitions of certain members of the British forces, at least after exposure to the relaxed moral atmosphere of the eastern Mediterranean. On one or two occasions since then, not least in the last few months, it has occurred to me that I was unduly stuffy all those years ago – that a healthy insurance claim (provided the crew did not go down with the ship) would have notably improved an intermittently rocky financial position in later life. In any event Basil would at the very least have been a useful technical adviser (to counteract a certain ingenious flying-officer) in a role I was to adopt a month or so later as LOLO, to which I shall shortly return. But this, through his own excess of enthusiasm, was not to be.

After calls at Seriphos, Yiaoura and Naxos came the turn of the delightful island of Paros – it was gratifying, of course, to visit, and in broad daylight, the main villages (as well as the more distant promontories) of islands with whose remoter beaches, only a few weeks back, I had been making briefer and more nervous contact. The entrance to Paros harbour, with the little town of Paroikia at the head of the bay, is unusually dramatic, since a scattering of precipitous rocks and islets lies close offshore. Years later I was nearly to exterminate myself and my family as I unwisely sought refuge in my little sloop *Stella Falcon* from a severe northerly gale there.

This time the weather was peaceful, and liberation from the enemy recent enough to warrant quite a crowd as we drew alongside the quay, the mayor himself being present and unleashing some warm words of welcome. I responded quite briefly but with equal warmth, after which, since we had had a longish passage, I retired to the cabin for a siesta. I had the place to myself for a change, since Basil, who had donned his full Welch Regiment uniform as we approached harbour, had disappeared silently and discreetly (as I thought) ashore.

After a couple of hours the Coxswain put his head down into the cabin and said 'You'd better come up on deck, skipper, there's a sort of deputation up here that wants to see you.' I staggered up to find an imposing ecclesiastical figure, the Abbot indeed of the famous monastery of Hekatompyliani, accompanied by sundry acolytes as well as by the mayor, this time in more sober mood. The Abbot addressed me in ringing tones and the formidably 'pure' dialect used by the Church, with the mayor interposing more demotic explanations from time to time. The gist of the complaint – since that was what, to my surprise, it turned out to be – was quite simple: that it was not fitting for a British officer, landed by a heroic British boat flying the White Ensign, to be seen parading round the streets of Paroikia in the company of four of the island's most notorious prostitutes. Would I please, as Capetanios, attempt to suppress this anomaly, which was causing offence to, and confusing the values of, all right-minded citizens?

I might have known that Basil's little run ashore would be less innocent than it had seemed – after all, the places we had visited since Syros had been too simple and too rustic to afford him the louche company he evidently required from time to time. Anyway, I made an apologetic speech in reply, claiming that this officer was (a) Army, (b) Welsh and (c) Greek, and promising to put a stop forthwith to his undesirable associations. Basil was, after all, very firmly under my command. The delegation withdrew, somewhat mollified, but I was left feeling distinctly dissatisfied with my companion and his effect on our mission. In fact by the time he arrived back on board, preening himself, thirty minutes later, I had worked myself into a bit of a rage, my essentially middle-class morality re-asserting itself after the ethical strains of Major Pope and the Syros scene. In short, I told the good Captain to pack his bags and beat it ashore, which is what he did – not without pathetic protests, perhaps justified in the circumstances, that he would be stranded there indefinitely, there being at that stage no regular communication between the island and the outside world. I replied that this was his affair, and that doubtless his powerful and disreputable friends would be able to arrange something. Actually (as he told me quite amicably when I encountered him in London many years later) he only had to wait a week or so, albeit in some discomfort, before finding some means of transport, slow and flea-ridden to be sure, back to the ancestral homelands of Chios.

Having no wish to linger in a place which, though beguiling enough, had been temporarily spoiled for us by this foolish social complication, I pressed onward to further islands on my list, the crew as glad as I to revert to a simpler all-naval status. Soon we found ourselves back in Keos, ten miles or so to the east of Cape Sounion and not too far from Athens itself. After doing my duty with lighthouses there I decided to extend my brief by paying a short visit to Phaleron Bay, only thirty or so miles away on the mainland to the north, and at least getting a distant view of the Acropolis itself.

We were about half way over there, admittedly a little confused over the exact position of enemy mine-fields and swept channels through them, when news over the radio put a stop to this junket. It became clear that the Communist guerrillas were now openly at war with the liberating British

183

forces, who had (as already hinted) been rather absent-minded over fully securing their positions in and around the capital. They could not quite believe (what intelligence reports and even our humble selves had been telling them for months) that EAM, the Communist political organisation behind ELAS, was determined to gain political control in Greece and throw out the monarchist and right-wing forces represented by the British Army and their accompanying Free Greek units from Egypt. So I sailed back to Syros to await instructions from Chios. It was not until well after Christmas (and Churchill's dramatic visit to Athens to see the Regent, Archbishop Makarios) that the situation around Athens was more or less under control again, and I was ordered to join the rest of the flotilla in Tourkolimano (now called Mikrolimano), the small-boat harbour on the edge of Phaleron Bay. There the other caiques were waiting to hand themselves over to the Greek Navy, which had decided in the end that it had a use for our boats before they were returned to their owners. I met up there with Ballantine, Fletcher, Thwaites, Turnbull, Barclay and co., and we had a whale of a time living not on board our boats but in the splendour of the Royal Hellenic Yacht Club, a low, white and rather glamorous building, providentially more or less undamaged, perched on the cliff above the harbour.

There we stayed for a couple of weeks, even after handing over the caiques themselves in an elaborate but excessively drab ceremony dominated by dour Greek naval officers and gorgeous-smelling priests. Solemn music was played by a military band and the caiques were drenched with holy water. Finally we were to instruct our Greek equivalents on the glories and limitations of our humble craft. My own successor, a mature figure, observed that he had been Captain of a merchant ship for many years, and hardly needed telling about how to run a simple fishing-boat. I took his point completely and left him to it, but he somehow got the wrong side of Stoker Peckham, who in a brief demonstration of the machinery failed to emphasise that we had no astern gear. The consequence was that, after a short proving-trip round

184

The monastery at Perissa in Santorin.

The crew of LS 12, and sacred Greeks. L/s King is bottom left.

185

the harbour, AHS 12 approached the quay at some speed. Orders of 'piso' (astern), given with increasing urgency, merely produced the close-shaven head of 'Stokes' from down below and the words 'okhi piso' ('no astern'), delivered in resigned and rather offended tones. I had stayed ashore during this exercise and heard the crash of collision with some perturbation. Senior Greek officers standing around were even more chagrined, though the damage done needed no more than a couple of days to repair. They took it out on my successor, and he on me, although, as I told him, I had offered to go over everything together in detail.

Staying on in the Yacht Club was truly delightful, especially since Athens had temporarily given itself over once again to gaiety and parties, to which young British naval officers had an almost automatic entrée. At the same time some fairly lavish counter-entertaining was being organised through the Coastal Force hierarchy now established in Turkolimano, whither the dubious Bill Toombs had moved as Commanding Officer of the Coastal Force Base from Castelorizo. Together with two other old Aegean hands called Frank Ramseyer and Martin Solomon (the latter an especially brave man and friend of Andy Lassen) he occupied, as his private residence, a house on the other side of the little bay from the Yacht Club. Certain business ventures were rapidly started up by this entrepreneurial trio, funded by and operated partly on behalf of the Royal Navy. One of these consisted in the systematic buying-up of postage stamps of the Occupation period. Then they acquired a large workshop that retreaded old motor tyres, as well as an ancient lighter that chugged all the way across the Aegean once a week to pick up coal. This commanded a high price on the Piraeus black market but was lying around, apparently belonging to no one in particular, on the dock-side at Chios. It was at their house (I think) that I first met Eleni, with whom I fell rapidly in love. I was not alone in this, since she was terribly pretty, with surprising cornflower-blue eyes, as well as being wonderfully vivacious and as nice as could possibly be. But I was fortunate – perhaps speaking some

Greek helped, although her English was pretty good, but it gave me a certain philhellenic *cachet* – and managed to gain her undivided attention.

During the handing-over celebrations I had met Commander Andreas Londos, who had been head of the second Anglo-Hellenic flotilla and now took charge of the whole group of boats, as well as fulfilling sundry other less well-defined duties of a marine kind. Impressed by my knowledge of Greek – which was growing day by day, especially at the more personal level – he suggested that I should attach myself to him as a kind of liaison officer. This I was entirely willing to do, since I was desperately keen to stay in or around Athens, partly for archaeological reasons and partly through an increasing and no less passionate obsession with Eleni, with whom I was having the most marvellous time, dancing in Athens and eating out in tavernas in Plaka and roaming the Acropolis late into the night. In those days it was all unenclosed, and the Parthenon by moonlight, which gleamed upwards from its polished marble paving-stones, could be wandered through at all hours. It seemed, somehow, to be moonlight most of the time. It was strange how few others, either Greek or British, took advantage of this wonderful opportunity; Eleni and I usually had the whole enchanted place to ourselves. The aromatic hill-sides below the great temples had a wholly different magic of their own, as we put off the hour of her return to her stepmother's house on the flanks of Lycabettus and mine to the sea at Tourkolimano – or, quite soon, to the Grande Bretagne hotel in the centre of Athens where I managed, by a certain degree of effrontery, to gain for myself a small room.

Being based in Constitution Square (which was not in those days choked with traffic) made my social life even more satisfying. The first few weeks of 1945 seemed to fly. I did all sorts of useful things (I hope) for Commander Londos, and soon became complacent enough to give myself an unofficial short title, LOLO, or Liaison Officer Londos. This was for local administrative convenience rather than self-aggrandisement – it saved time with the interminable signals that had to be sent to and fro within the Piraeus area, and to which I was in any case temperamentally allergic. But it was, undoubtedly, an act of *hubris* that brought its own downfall, with the help (as I suspected) of Flying Officer Martin-Trigona, whose earlier presence as stores officer in our Turkish bases has already been noted. He was lurking around in Piraeus somehow and suddenly started making himself useful to my Greek master, who needed to build up his reputation by acquiring all sorts of stores which lay completely beyond my ken. Triggy, it was rumoured, had managed to gain illegal possession of a British Army jeep and a 15-hundredweight truck and make them over to the Greek Navy, or rather to the Londos bit of it. This was undeniably a valuable service, and suddenly I ceased to be quite so popular. A message on some technical matter had to be sent down from Greek naval headquarters to FOLEM (Flag Officer, Levant and Eastern Mediterranean) in Alexandria; it gratuitously, or so I thought, contrived to suggest that some minor but controversial course of action had been authorized by LOLO. The result, not long delayed, was inevitable, and must surely have been foreseen – an urgent signal from FOLEM to higher naval authority in Piraeus which simply asked the following pregnant question: 'Who is LOLO?' The answer, 'Sub-Lieutenant G. S. Kirk, RNV(S)R', evidently failed to impress. A further signal was received by return to the effect that Sub-Lieutenant Kirk had better report immediately, repeat *immediately*, to the naval base in Alexandria.

The idyll, in short, was temporarily at an end, at least in its LOLO form. That was peculiarly frustrating, since together with Eleni, and another couple with whom we were friendly – he my friend from Beirut and before that from HMS King Alfred called Don Smith, who possessed a jeep – I had recently been able to explore the countryside and the antiquities outside Athens. Kephissia had revealed its semi-rural delights and we had even spent an agreeable night or two in the vicinity of ancient Corinth. Now all that was at an end, owing to my stupidity as well as my deficient powers as inter-services scavenger and entrepreneur compared with the accomplished Triggy. For this was not at all my métier – I had confined myself to more regular naval liaison – and I was perhaps lucky to last so long. Commander Londos was outwardly sympathetic at my removal, but there was nothing to be done. He was a pragmatic man, impressive enough in his way and father of two lovely young daughters; apart from everything else I was sorry to leave him. He temporarily recruited Triggy to his staff; soon he went into politics and became the first ever Greek Minister of Tourism, in which capacity I was to meet him again some three years later.

Arrival in Alex could have been worse. I was severely put on the mat for tampering with the sacred institution of short titles, as well as for occupying for several weeks a wholly mythical job to which I had not been appointed. Pleading administrative naiveté and excessive philhellenism, I was then treated with the same detached kind of put-down as had been meted out to other members of the flotilla, which was perhaps thought by this time, in certain quarters, to have become too uppity. Higher authority tended to write about our activities, when it happened to hear of them, with enthusiasm, but there was a certain type of shore-based officer to whom we were undoubtedly an irritant – once, that is, the glamour of 'up in the islands' could no longer be made to reflect in some way upon themselves.

After all, we had for many months behaved with fairly total disregard of normal naval channels, especially in the requisitioning of stores for our boats and in demands for exceptional activity in the slothful and corrupt world of the Beirut repair-yards. Then again the demon rum, that index of tight nautical procedures, was issued in jars to our caiques more or less on request, from one of the supply schooners, it being assumed that life in a good deal of fresh air, and the need to placate visiting Turks and the like, made it impracticable to count up tots per man per day. Actually a regular daily rum ration was not flotilla practice, partly perhaps

189

because of the natural *joie de vivre* of some of our excellent if irregular sailors but also because we young officers had not been too keen on the system during our own time as ratings. Similarly, gold sovereigns were carried on board in quantities that probably irked Pursers and the like back in Alex and Beirut. There had been virtually no abuse of these privileges, but now the time had come to see that these young Sub-Lieutenants conformed more fully in these and other matters. Such other matters included clothing (since our modified disregard of regulation uniform did not go down well in places like Alexandria), public respect for all shore-based officers (since we had lost the habit of rapid and automatic saluting), and obedience to the Royal Navy's more hallowed signal procedures. We were duly appointed, therefore, to various unexotic, or even demeaning, posts. Albert Priestly, for instance, an admittedly eccentric young Yorkshireman who had married a Turkolimano lady and later had a short and erratic career with the Customs Service, was put in charge of the Water Boat in Alexandria harbour. As for me, I was given command of a mine-sweeping ML based in the northern Aegean, whither I was ordered to proceed without delay.

This particular appointment could (I suppose) have been judged malicious rather than demeaning, containing a certain punitive element in response to my agreeable fantasies as LOLO. For the facts were, first, that mine-sweeping was a skilled technique; second, that it could be dangerous; third, that I knew absolutely nothing about it. A mild suggestion that I might be sent on a short course to acquire the more rudimentary training required was dismissed in a delightfully care-free manner: 'Oh, it's pretty easy with an ML, old boy, you just chuck out a paravane, isn't it? and cut the bloody wire.' So, glad to be returning without delay to Greek waters, but without much in the way of real enthusiasm for this particular nautical function, I caught an RAF Dakota to Athens for onward routing from there.

Was it on that flight that the pilot obligingly circled the Acropolis at about five hundred feet? At any rate I felt queasy in two different ways: first through a sudden quite intense panic about whether we could stay in the air, the result I believe of a lingering and unsuspected uneasiness over the earlier flight by Dakota from England to Cairo; and second because I was feeling distinctly peculiar in any case. I have forgotten where I spent the first night after landing, but I was evidently running quite a high fever and next day saw a doctor who promptly consigned me to a ramshackle military hospital near the airport, along the coast road towards Sounion. 'Atypical pneumonia' was temporarily unpleasant but not very serious, responding slowly to the occasional aspirin (the only drug available in that hospital at the time), a nightly tot of whisky diverted from a surgical ward, and a daily dozen of snails collected for me on her way to work by a motherly Greek nurse. The greatest personal impact of this short interlude of ill-health was that, as with the hole dug for the Anderson shelter in my parents' garden some five years before, it fortuitously saved me from probable extinction. Some other poor devil had to take over the mine-sweeping ML up north, and it blew up quite quickly, within days rather than weeks. Fortunately I knew, and know, no more than that. It is, I suppose, theoretically possible, but unlikely, that my own complete ignorance of mine-sweeping techniques, combined with a certain close attention to detail where matters of life and limb were concerned, might have been safer, rather than more dangerous, for all concerned.

When I emerged from hospital the good life started all over again, not to be seriously interrupted when I received a fresh appointment, this time to the command of HDML 1004 – which was not, I was pleased to learn, equipped for mine-sweeping, and was based on the Coastal Force outfit in Tourkolimano. At this stage of the war only one officer was carried aboard those smaller MLs, so this did not signify a promotion exactly; but it was nice to be on my own, I did not have to cope with mines, and it was rather fun to whizz round at the great speed of eleven knots – still grotesquely slow, but better than the caique's steady six. Slowness apart, those

HDMLs were absolutely delightful vessels, comfortable for officer and crew, good-looking, and excellent sea-boats for their size. There was a capacious wheel-house which made navigation and conning the boat a pleasure, and where one was well-sheltered in bad weather. The wardroom was a comfortable little place, especially for one, with varnished mahogany and polished brass giving it a respectable and homely air. Indeed this particular little space, together with that of my yacht *Stella Falcon*'s mahogany and iroko-lined cabin twenty years later, was among the three or four most soothing and beautiful I have ever occupied. Perhaps that reflects a sub-conscious predilection for small, womb-like enclosures? I think not; but in any event I used greatly to enjoy a civilized glass of sherry there, absolutely necessary indeed to make my lunch palatable – the cooking on board being necessarily better than on LS 12, but not exactly refined or even easily digestible, given that one spent less time nowadays getting sloshed by spray in the healthy open air.

Our duties included visiting various islands for various administrative purposes, some useful, some apparently futile. It was now March or April, and there was still bad weather to be encountered. At this stage of the war the need for blasting through the night into short and uncomfortable head seas did not seem quite so imperative. On one such occasion I turned back to Piraeus, about three hours after leaving at the inconvenient and unnecessary time of 8 p.m., with a mildly blown main gasket. Lieutenant-Commander Toombs, never at his best at that time of evening, was not pleased, and ordered the chief motor-mechanic at the base to change the gasket in person and send me off again before midnight. Perhaps I should interject that I had annoyed my senior officer, a couple of weeks before, by sending a rather peremptory request that only *relevant* signals be repeated to ML 1004; my mornings were being made a nightmare by nautical junk mail that was overflowing from my capacious wastepaper basket. That resulted in an urgent summons ashore and a more or less public dressing-down, not unreasonable perhaps in the circumstances. Anyway, by this time it was close to 11 p.m., and the Chief, though theoretically still on duty, seemed awfully sleepy, if not positively blotto. What happened next was that he fell asleep while leaning on a power-drill with which he was fiddling about trying to loosen the cylinder-head, and contrived to drill a neat hole into the guts of the engine. For some reason ML 1004 had American Packard engines, not the standard British ones, and getting a whole new cylinder-head from the States took all of three weeks. Toombs fumed at the temporary loss of one of his craft, I expressed great sorrow and frustration, but was stoically prepared to console myself once more with the cultural possibilities of life ashore and the company of beautiful Eleni. My crew, I hasten to add, were little less delighted.

I managed to see little more of Toombs after that, and it was not until a year or two later that news became widely known of his final departure from Greek waters. Apparently he had stayed on in Piraeus after demobilization, no doubt directing in a purely civilian capacity the various rackets with which he had been connected before. He had also acquired a yacht and a lady-friend, both relatively exotic. One evening as sundowners were being consumed on the balcony of his house above the harbour the yacht was observed motoring unexpectedly out to sea. On investigation the lady-friend, too, was missing, together with one of the henchmen and a great many gold sovereigns. Toombs himself, evidently caught by surprise, set off with all speed on a pursuit that was presumably unsuccessful, and that seemed to have led to his total disappearance from the face of the earth. Or did he return eventually to New Zealand whence he sprang? The truth may be less glamorous, since I learned quite recently from Adrian Seligman that he had run into Toombs years later in Cyprus, where he had got into some kind of trouble working as a clerk at the Army base there. Yet the whole Toombs career had an unmistakably mythical aura, and I cannot help suspecting an eventual ending more truly god-like, or perhaps demonic, than that.

Be that as it may, he had now been obliged to despatch ML 1004 and three other similar boats for final paying-off in Malta. It was late summer of 1945 and the war was coming to an end. I, like others who had been part-way through a university course earlier on, was given accelerated demobilization in order to resume my studies. Just before that happened I was tentatively offered the job of Flag-Lieutenant to the Admiral commanding Greek waters. There was a strong temptation to accept, but on the other hand I was keen to take my degree and get started on a career. Promotion to Lieutenant had just come through (the Navy having the great merit of doing such things by age and after due lapse of time), and I felt that, much as I admired the Royal Navy as a whole, I had seen almost enough of it. The thought also occurred that a certain independence of mind developed during the last year or so might not go down too well with Admirals and the like. On a personal level, Athens was still delightful in its way, but I felt that I should find myself permanently attached to Eleni if I stayed around much longer. That was a delightful prospect, but like many young people at the end of the war I wanted freedom of every kind, just for the time being, in order to take a look round and make unhurried choices for the future. Arriving back home with a foreign wife, especially while still a student, really seemed out of the question. I am not saying that this way of looking at things was particularly sensible (I have often regretted it since), rather that it is more or less what happened. So I said a temporary goodbye to Eleni – she would be able to visit England in a few months – and headed off with the other three boats to Malta, by way of Corfu, southern Italy and Sicily.

The voyage was uneventful but poignant; I was truly devastated to be leaving Greek waters. Some consolation was offered by the staggering sight of the lights of Italy and Sicily. Sailing by night was completely transformed, since the lighthouses and light-buoys around the Messina channel and down the west coast of Sicily had been restored far more quickly, and were in any case more brilliant and much more profuse, than those in the Aegean and around Greece. The effect could be almost blinding to those used only to poking around in darker waters. Perhaps it was that that caused us to be careless in entering Sybaris, second home of Pythagoras – or rather being too relaxed once we were secured alongside in the soulless modern harbour there. The little boys of southern Italy were not slow to reveal their talents: within an hour of mooring alongside we had mysteriously lost a large stern hawser, which had been quietly and efficiently filched, allowing the boat to swing out from the quay. Within a further hour there was a mass raid of about five youngsters on one of the deck stowage-lockers beside the bridge, from which further ropes were removed. This time the malefactors were seen and almost caught, but the Coxswain, who was directing the pursuit, suddenly seemed to lose enthusiasm, remarking darkly that ill winds had their uses. What this meant was that, when we came to de-store a few days later in Malta, a remarkable proportion of the things we could not account for – lost, no doubt, ages before, and carelessly signed for by me when I took over the boat – turned out to have been stored in that huge port locker and pillaged by the fierce bandits of Sybaris.

Malta was soulless and barren, the process of decommissioning no less so, and I was heartily relieved, by the end of September 1945, after just over four years in the Navy, to be heading back to the more intellectual rigours of life in Cambridge once again. What I did not realize at the time was that one of the most dramatic as well as the most fulfilling epochs of my life was coming to an end – one that cast a glow, admittedly, upon regular long trips to Greece in years to come, at least until that, too, faded for a while under the deadly impact of mass tourism.

HDML 1004.

Captain Anders Lassen, V.C.

CHAPTER 13

Back to Cambridge, and

Archaeology in Athens

Leaving the Services, for a Reserve Officer, was a pallid affair. No kindly Admiral waved goodbye or pressed on one the equivalent of a gold watch. Campaign medals would arrive many months later, unattractively crammed into a small cardboard box. One simply reported at an anonymous hangar somewhere in North London – or was it Earl's Court? – to queue for a de-mob suit. From the limited styles on offer I chose one of the worst, a chalk-striped blue number which, as my father was not slow to point out, was strictly unwearable by any would-be gent. As a rite of passage the proceedings were a mirror-image of the issue of bell-bottoms and the rest of Jolly Jack Tar's rig at Butlin's in Skegness some four years before. Much had changed in the interval, but those of us who had survived needed, once again, a fresh mentality and a different pair of trousers. The ceremonial correspondences were striking, perhaps inevitable. Could they have been planned by some resident naval anthropologist deep in Queen Anne's Mansions? Probably not; but in any case that, so far as I can remember, was that, and after a flying visit home to see my parents I proceeded in haste to Cambridge, where the Michaelmas Term had just begun.

To my disappointment I was again given rooms in Clare's featureless Memorial Court, though at least they were on the first floor and not (as in my previous undergraduate incarnation) the ground floor, thus justifying the occasional after-hours climb-in. In those days we had to be back in college by midnight, unless special permission had been granted. That sort of rule was a bit galling to those of us just out of the Services, accustomed to throwing our weight about, giving orders, being saluted and all that. In the Levant Schooners there had been relatively little pomp and ceremony, but afterwards in Athens, especially in my self-imposed role as LOLO, I had grown used to throwing off the odd salute – and even to receiving the occasional one in return. It was indeed quite difficult to change from being an officer to being an other-rank, so to speak; especially as it took a couple of weeks to kit oneself out again in civilian clothes (de-mob suit notwithstanding), and so discard one's nice uniform – something I remember doing with great reluctance. The college porters helped us to adjust by being mildly deferential to the newly de-commissioned ones among us. The dons, on the other hand, rightly took no notice of pretensions acquired elsewhere, and expected us to buckle to and behave once again like nice young adolescents.

In my freshman year at Clare, over four years back, there had been almost no dons around; now there were almost too many. Most of those who had re-appeared seemed stuffy and unattractive. The college had more than its share of scientists and engineers, who were said to reserve their more animated conversations for the laboratory. But there was at least one startling exception; for my own teacher was to be N. G. L. Hammond, just back from years of courageous war service in occupied Greece, highly decorated with the DSO. Here was a man to do away with self-aggrandizement or self-pity, one that understood some of the minor problems of the demobilized undergraduate, and perhaps even had equivalent ones of his own; although I doubt that, since he had returned to a delightful wife and family and a pleasant house, Merton Cottage on Queens' Road. I had not, of course, met him until now, since he had already been away in occupied Greece during my first student year. Now he at once endeared himself by his informal and no-nonsense manner and his professional approach to teaching. Nick Hammond was liked by everyone;

at the same time he was not the usual wishy-washy sort of popular don – not at all the kind of person one wished to displease by showing up a shoddy essay or arriving late for a supervision. His own lack of pretension helped one shed the last tatters of OLQ or 'officer-like qualities', once so much sought after and now so irrelevant. At last I felt I had a teacher of H. W. White calibre (though so totally different in personality and physique) for whom I could exert myself properly once again.

The only drawback was that he was primarily an ancient historian, whereas I wanted to specialize (for Part II of the Classical Tripos) in ancient philosophy – fresh as I was from the land of Socrates and feeling certain that I was no historian in the more technical sense, politics, military history and all that. This meant that some of my specialized supervisions (the Cambridge term for tutorials) were taught by others, with Nick Hammond accounting for the rest. At any rate I wrote him a weekly essay, 15 or 20 pages of fairly serious stuff, on Greek and Latin literature, the central core of a Classical education, as well as on historical topics that I could not entirely avoid. He used to work through these essays very seriously – none of that ambivalent Oxford practice of the pupil reading them aloud! – and fill the margins with pertinent queries and massive additional information. Discussion afterwards was pointed and practical. He was not a man who liked persiflage, indeed his own approach to literary and philosophical matters was a fairly concrete one. That was perhaps something I did not particularly need, being a mildly concrete character (neuroses apart) myself. A more abstract or even aesthetic approach might have been productive. But he was first-rate at getting one going again, at clearing away the rust of four years' absence and thrusting one wholesale into the problems of a different world, the ancient one I mean. If this splendid man had a weakness it was that *in those days* (for by some years later things had entirely changed) he was not a very exciting lecturer. That may be unfair, since in any case a certain blandness, amounting at times to extreme dullness, was characteristic of many or even most Classical lecturers in Cambridge at that period.

The question of lecturing became even more important when I myself later joined the profession, and I reflect from time to time on my models, both bad and good. Four years earlier, D. S. Robertson, the Regius Professor of Greek, had been intermittently compulsive in a rather dry way on early Greek poetry. Another Trinity don, A. S. F. Gow, likewise an Anglicized Scot, had held our attention by terrifying learning on the subject of Theocritus. This was a famous and oft-repeated course held in a dingy lecture-room at that revered college, of which the high point was supposed (by the students, that is, who are perennially silly over this kind of thing) to be his demonstration of a magical device, the 'bull-roarer', alluded to by the poet. Personally I found the occasion a bit of an anti-climax, and was more entranced by the side-whiskers and generally Victorian demeanour of an unusual man (collector of Degas drawings and friend of the deplorable Anthony Blunt) whom I came to know well in the last two years of his long life. Otherwise that first year's lecturing (except for a short extra-curricular series, on relativity no less, by Bertrand Russell) had been not exactly electrifying. But then, like many undergraduates, I simply didn't know enough at the time to look out for the teachers of real distinction, like the eminent Platonist F. M. Cornford, also of Trinity as it happens.

That had been in my first undergraduate year. During this second and last one in 1945–6 (for wartime regulations allowed me to complete the Tripos in two much-separated doses) things were not much better. Professor Hackforth was sound but unexciting on Plato; he had a disconcerting habit of casting oblique glances, at the rate of almost exactly one a minute, into the furthermost upper corner of the lecture-room. W. K. C. Guthrie, who was to be Hackforth's successor in the Laurence Chair of Ancient Philosophy, was mellifluous on Aristotle but not hard-edged enough to make this compelling thinker quite real. Then on early Greek thinkers, those

'Presocratics' who were to become an important concern of mine in subsequent years, we had F. H. Sandbach – 'we' being quite a small group of ancient philosophy specialists, no more than a dozen or so, including two delightful girls, Rosemary Lloyd and Jean Stiven. Others doing Part II, but with different special interests, included my eventual successor in the Regius Chair, E. W. Handley, and John Chadwick of Linear B fame.

Harry Sandbach was a lovable figure, a distinguished scholar in both Greek and Latin, who many years later became a friend and mentor and to whom John Raven and I dedicated our book *The Presocratic Philosophers* when it came out in 1957. I think it can fairly be said that he was at that time a rather *incomprehensible* lecturer, partly no doubt because of his subject, which is quite a complex one. That is, one has to reconstruct the thought of these primitive but brilliant thinkers partly from occasional and fragmentary quotations in much later Greek writers, partly from Aristotle's dry and sometimes unsympathetic references to them, and partly from summaries of treatises on the history of physics and theology by his pupil Theophrastus. In addition, Sandbach was much concerned at the time with a running dispute, which afforded us constant amusement, between himself and an Italian scholar of lesser genius. At any rate he did not really succeed in making this difficult branch of Greek studies wholly intelligible – in fact we occasionally sat through the whole fifty minutes of a lecture without taking in anything much at all. But he did not obliterate the brilliant lustre of these thinkers, and that was a great merit. We became fascinated by them, and I formed an early determination to improve on the stolid German handbook, 'Ritter and Preller', in which the main evidence for them was unattractively presented, partly in Latin, for student use.

It was a difficult year in a way, and I never managed to recapture even the modified glamour of undergraduate Cambridge that my first year there had provided. Social life was restricted, partly because I missed Eleni and the whole romantic background of Greece. But I worked hard, and looked to the future. There were, of course, new friendships to be made; Michael Kerr, likewise at Clare, has remained one of the closest. Son of Alfred Kerr the German dramatic critic, he was incarcerated in the Isle of Man as a small boy, went into the RAF and then to the Bar, ending as a Lord Justice of Appeal, a brilliant feat. Through the years he has helped me with good advice, not all of which I have had the chance to follow, let alone reciprocate.

As the months moved on and the Tripos approached I became more and more conscious that during my several years' absence from the academic scene I had lost my old taste for – and effortless way of dealing with – examinations. By the time mid-May arrived, my old bugbear hay-fever (which had left me altogether while I was in the Mediterranean) returned with a vengeance, exacerbated no doubt by nervous tension and turning into quite severe asthma at night, which I reluctantly learned to subdue with strong drafts of Scotch. But there were only eleven three-hour papers to be got through, and somehow, despite lack of sleep and the occasional hangover, I survived, emerging with a good First and now having to face up seriously to a choice of career.

Already, before the Tripos, I had had some kind of preliminary interview for the Foreign Service, also (at the behest of the university appointments board) with Shell. Neither had made a startling impression, the latter requiring that I should begin with a couple of years in Venezuela, which struck me at the time as a deeply repellent prospect. Now, in contrast, it was clear that an academic career was within my immediate grasp if I chose. Events moved fast. As soon as the Tripos results were out – in those days the lists were solemnly recited in the Senate House by the Chairman of Examiners before being posted on the notice-boards outside – I received a note asking me to call on the Reverend Martin Charlesworth, a jovial prelate and respected lecturer in ancient history (again!) in St John's College. There he plied me with sherry and tried his best to persuade me to accept a junior post in the Classics department at Manchester University, for which he held some kind of watching brief. Manchester seeming as remote as Venezuela, I politely but firmly declined. On returning to my rooms in Clare I found another note waiting for me, this time from the Vice-Master of Trinity Hall, with a specific offer of a Research Fellowship there. This, I thought, was to be taken more seriously – I did not, after all, really want to leave Cambridge – and I talked it over with Nick Hammond. The difficulty was that I didn't feel any overwhelming vocation for *teaching*; although ancient Greece was still a major concern and the thought of getting deeper into the Presocratics was powerfully attractive. Hammond suggested, reasonably enough, that perhaps the fascination with teaching would come later. Up to a point it did, but I never fully developed that passion for transferring my own knowledge and perceptions into other people's minds that is a crucial element of the true vocation. Partly, at least, that was the result of a basic and continuing scepticism about my own knowledge and understanding – a self-doubt which, commendably Socratic though it might be, was one which (as I subsequently noticed) most successful teachers, whatever their state of information or intelligence, simply do not possess.

Anyway, Trinity Hall, for three years at least, it turned out to be, and I moved with gratifying rapidity from being an undergraduate to being a don. 'The Hall' was a relatively small college, next door as it happens to Clare College, with no more than fourteen Fellows at the time and less than a hundred and fifty undergraduates. It was best known for law and rowing, neither of which at all interested me (the former, perhaps, because I still faintly regretted that I had not chosen, or been encouraged by my father, to practise it myself); on the other hand it had a good reputation as a 'nice college'. The Classics don (who was also Vice-Master, the one who had written to me) was a distinctly odd bird, the Reverend C. F. Angus, a Nonconformist minister of Scottish descent whose Christianity seemed to be mainly sublimated Plato. I had only recently sat through his lectures on Plato's *Phaedo*. They were striking for their highly emotional tone and the evident dedication, to the point of extreme credulity, of the lecturer, who seemed to believe everything Plato made Socrates say, including virtually all of his arguments for the immortality of the soul – which, for all the Platonic genius, range from the distinctly dicey to the metaphysically bizarre.

Since it was C. F. Angus, as I supposed, who had initiated my election to a Fellowship, I was always respectful and duly grateful to him; but never got on to close terms, disliking the patronizing manner – together with the Socratic appearance, snub-nose and all – that was evidently so tolerable to many undergraduates at the time and made his reading parties in Morthoe (why?) a curiously popular annual event. He was famous for carrying on deep conversations in his rooms with student friends until all hours – about what, I do not precisely know, although his deep streak of Christian Platonism or Platonic Christianity underlay much of it, evidently soothing the troubled psyches of those who talked with him late into the night. On his side, no doubt, those friendships with young people helped to ease the loneliness and frustration of a rather introverted bachelor, one who never achieved all that he was capable of as a scholar and who late in life spent too many hours on an indifferent verse translation, never completed, of the poet Lucretius. Probably I am unfair to those midnight conversations – some of his pupils claimed to have been greatly helped, as well as totally enthralled, by them.

In those days no fewer young people than now had problems of adjustment, of growing up, of sexuality, of learning to live by themselves; and Cambridge always had its self-professed experts in dealing with them. Some of these were better at stirring up trouble than at calming it down, and I suspect Angus of belonging to this group. At all events the incidence of mildly disturbed students seemed to decline after his demise, when a succession of excellent college chaplains provided more straightforward aid of a simpler Christian kind. Some confirmation was provided by the case of David Balme, Classics don at Jesus College, to whom I had gone for Aristotle supervisions and whom I greatly liked. I asked him to dinner in college, and it was at once obvious that he and Angus deeply mistrusted each other. David had evidently come within the magic circle when he was an undergraduate, and quickly extricated himself from it. When he joined the RAF, Angus opined to all and sundry that he was wholly unsuitable for active service, a very nervous and insecure character. He was not, I think, best pleased when David turned into an ace bomber pilot, winning the DSO and DFC. On the other hand a much less complex character than David, though equally likable, had also joined in the late-night sessions and even, I think, went on at least one Morthoe party; his reaction to the latter-day Socrates was one of deep, and to me quite astounding, veneration. That was my first father-in-law, Ralph Traill, an extremely lovable if not a very theoretical man, who read medicine not at Trinity Hall but at Trinity and came into the Angus orbit because he too, but ten years or so later, had been at Charterhouse School.

Life in my new college was very pleasant for the first year. I had a stipend of £300 a year, together with rooms that were comfortable, if not lavish, in an undistinguished 1930s block. Yet they seemed spacious enough to me at the time, especially in comparison with my minute cabin in LS 12 or the more gracious affair in HDML 1004; and they looked down towards the River Cam. High Table food was a revelation after the institutionalized diet served to the undergraduates of Clare, and I much enjoyed the marvellous wines which accompanied dinner. What I did not enjoy was the port-drinking ritual afterwards, when as Junior Fellow it was my duty to pass round decanters and biscuits and so on (quite unnecessarily) and then listen to boring conversation from my elders and betters when I could have been back in my rooms working on Heraclitus or, a newly developed passion, listening to music. There were a couple of other young Fellows around, Bernard Neal and George Kenner, and they felt much the same. Admittedly, among our older colleagues there were some ripe and rewarding figures, who dined, however, only once a week. One was Professor Gutteridge, a law don of enormous girth and rubicund countenance, a truly Dickensian figure much given to taking snuff, amiable and entertaining. Another was Louis Clarke, a rich and delightful bachelor who had just been appointed, at a fairly advanced age, as Director of the Fitzwilliam Museum – a post he accepted, as he told me later, on the advice of his psychiatrist. His conversation was hard to follow, but lively and uninhibited, curiously punctuated by small shrieks. He asked us younger ones regularly to his house for marvellous dinners. When we were shown around on one occasion I could not help noticing that he kept a couple of admittedly small Leonardo drawings (one, I remember, of an ermine) in the second spare bedroom, which I considered rather grand. Louis was not an especially academic person – perhaps an advantage in his particular post – but he had marvellous taste and feeling for furniture, paintings and decorative objects, and the Fitzwilliam took on a new charm under his direction. His wealth came from coal mines in Northumberland, and his views on financial matters were no less conservative than those of Professor Gutteridge. All financial items on the agenda at college meetings tended to produce a curious kind of concerted rumble from the two of them, seated invariably side by side, in which the words 'Blue Chip' were a dominant element. They were keen on railway shares, and together with the college Bursar, a well-known law Fellow called J. W. C. Turner, had presided over a marked decline in the college's income during the recent war – a feat achieved (as I learned later) by no other Cambridge college.

The legal eminence of Trinity Hall had its drawbacks. Academic lawyers in those days tended not to be particularly scintillating in conversation, and I could sympathize with the malicious comment that was sometimes made (and is not, I am sure, wholly true) that all the bright lawyers went to practice at the Bar, leaving the less bright ones to become dons. One of my three legal colleagues at the time was a Welshman much beloved of his students, largely, so far as I could see, because he offered them unsuitable quantities of drink when they went for supervision. He had an unending fund of dirty stories which he told over and over again, to my extreme tedium, when I sat next to him after High Table dinner. I have not generally found such tales amusing, not through any particular sexual stuffiness (all that having been more or less knocked out of one in the Navy), but because the tales themselves are generally predictable and their dedicated tellers self-conscious, furtive, boring or otherwise awful. Anyway, for this and other reasons I started not 'coming through', that is, to the Combination Room for port and dessert, on many nights when I had dined. This eventually produced a rebuke from the Vice-Master, who told me that it was my positive duty to show up on a regular basis after Hall. This was very silly and I should have taken no notice. As it was, I dined out more often, elevated my reservations concerning the Reverend C. F. Angus a degree further, and decided that my days as a college Fellow were probably in any case numbered.

There were, however, strong compensations in the way of companionship. Soon after I was made a Fellow, Graham Storey was taken on as English don, and he was excellent company; so too was Shaun Wylie, fresh out of Bletchley Park and that rare being an articulate and amusing mathematician. An older friend was Launcelot Fleming, who was the college Dean (later becoming Bishop of Portsmouth and Norwich and Chaplain to the Queen). We younger ones played squash with him and mercilessly exploited his curious inability to sweat, which at crucial moments reduced him to a kind of physical collapse and allowed us to win. One winter he invited us up for a week to his grand family house on the shores of Loch Rannoch, where the days were spent in fell-walking (and on one occasion a stumbling bout of deer-stalking) and the evenings in Scottish dancing in his or neighbouring houses. That was my closest contact with aristocratic Scottishness, and I must say I greatly enjoyed it, though no doubt it could become too much of a good thing. Launcelot once preached in chapel on the subject of cynicism, telling George Kenner and myself beforehand, rather sweetly, that

207

the sermon was really directed, in the nicest possible way, against ourselves. We did not, of course, turn up to hear it. Cynicism required that of us at the very least, though we both regretted that we could not give additional pleasure to a great and good man.

Back in Cambridge I was trying, a trifle absent-mindedly perhaps, to choose between the attractions of two or three different girl-friends, partly in order to divert my thoughts from Eleni back there in Athens. The trouble was that I liked, in one way or another, practically all girls. Fortunately I was neither confident nor ruthless enough to put my liking into very immediate effect. I had met an extremely beautiful Swedish girl at a dinner-party given by Helen and Lawrence Fowler; her name was deceptively English, Mildred Johnson, but she was in Cambridge to learn that tongue. For a time I held her various pursuers at bay; she came to stay at my home in Bramcote, I remember, rather to my parents' surprise, for they could see that she was a rich girl and probably beyond my horizon. When she left England I was driven down in the company Rolls-Royce to see her off at Tilbury, and for over a year afterwards sent her unhappy letters to which she very seldom, and very lovingly, replied. Thereafter she retreated into the world of Swedish shipping and high life, becoming managing director of her family shipping company, the biggest in Sweden, Johnson Brothers. Not too long ago I saw a gleaming white ship bearing her name in a Cretan harbour, and it reminded me of the agony of waiting in vain for letters from her when, in the autumn of 1947, I became a Student of the British School at Athens.

For my work on Heraclitus of Ephesus was well under way, and it was time to broaden scholarly horizons. Normally at this stage a neophyte scholar would take off for Germany for a year, both to make direct contact with German scholars – in the forefront of Classical research for so long – and to learn their language properly. But in late 1947 that was not so easy. Germany was still in a mess, its university apparatus hardly put together again. I did not need much persuading to decide on Greece instead. Greece still had an almost sacred attraction for me, and there I could come to closer grips with the intriguing mysteries of archaeology, with which I had made those first thrilling contacts near the monastery of Perissa in wartime Santorin, and then after a night in Turkish custody at Didyma – not to speak of the moonlit Acropolis, and then Old Corinth, in the company of Eleni. And so I arranged to go out to the British School of Archaeology in Athens, now opening to post-graduate students for the first time since 1939. The prospect was an exciting one which entirely set aside any lingering concern about improving my German; especially since a certain lack of enthusiasm, natural enough in the circumstances, manifested itself for the land of one's recent enemies.

And yet, though the year was to be a fruitful one, I might have done better to break my way into Germany after all. Apart from greater facility with the language itself, I might have acquired more of a taste for learned footnotes and exuberant bibliography. As it is, I persisted in avoiding the former where possible and cutting down on the latter. This has, perhaps, given my published work a kind of clarity, at the cost of sometimes suggesting to critics a certain disdain for other people's opinions – which is not, I believe, true, unless those opinions are palpably secondhand or manifestly wrong. At all events I continue to despise unnecessary footnotes – and many footnotes in many subjects *are* just that. Greek studies may be a special case, since they have been carried on so minutely and for so many hundreds of years; but it is hard to overlook that footnotes even in that particular field are often concerned with meticulous allusion to other scholars' mistakes – or with ideas that might be better left, with their benighted authors, to lapse into oblivion.

To be in Athens again was in any case delightful. The British School of Archaeology is in Kolonaki, then a pleasant suburb overlooking Mount Hymettus (its stony flanks violet at sunset) – now even those streets are choked with cars and the view southward over the School gardens is blocked by a

209

towering new (but already crumbling) wing of the Evanghelismos hospital. Normally the students would have lived in the hostel, a stolid building which also housed the library; but for this first year there were only three of us, of varying and untypical degrees of seniority, and we were lodged in the Director's house itself.

We made, undoubtedly, a strange trio. One was Sylvia Benton, an elderly and remarkable Scotswoman of ferocious appearance, originally a schoolteacher, who had excavated the Polis bay cave in Ithaca just before the war – a small dig but a dramatic one. The second was Helen Thomas (now Lady Waterhouse), a few years older than me and who like Sylvia had pre-war experience of Greece, a tough and sympathetic figure, a Mycenaean specialist. The third of course was myself, brash and youthful-looking, rather weedy perhaps, at any rate by contrast. Our clothes-sense at that time was of a strictly practical persuasion: I wore a seedy panama sun-hat (later discovered to be black in essence, but painted white), but it was Sylvia that made the three of us look distinctly peculiar *en masse* as we made our ritual weekly excursion down to Constitution Square to draw money from American Express. With her fierce eyes, hawk-like nose usually burned to a dull crimson, straggling grey hair and striking head-gear she impressed the Athenians no end, so much so that passers-by could occasionally be seen covertly crossing themselves, something Sylvia herself seemed not to notice.

The Director's house was charming, an unpretentious neo-classical building set among pine-trees, with the American School, equally pleasant, just next door and sharing the same shady garden, which contained a battered tennis-court. The Director himself was J. M. Cook, a Kingsman by origin, and I was fortunate to spend this year under his aegis. Many years later I was to become, for a short time, a professorial colleague of his at Bristol. He was a delightful man with a quizzical sense of humour, and his wife Enid, a capable and charming Scotswoman, kept a sharp motherly eye on us all. John was devoted to Greece and its antiquities, about which he seemed to know almost everything. He did not at all mind sharing his knowledge, and I only regret now that I spent so much time in the School library and so relatively little time sitting at his feet. At week-ends, at least, we would all pile into the School jeep to go for an *ekdrome*, an excursion to some ancient site, usually with a stop for a bathe somewhere on the way. Once I went off for a week with John and Enid and their son Michael, then aged three. The objective was the bare island of Kythnos, where much pleasant meandering over the steep aromatic hillsides, with the other islands of the group, Seriphos, Siphnos and Keos, gleaming in the purple seas beyond and below us, was accomplished in search of sherd-scatters as a sign of ancient Dark-Age habitation. John, who had dug at Perachora before the war under Humfrey Payne, was particularly good on sherds (as also on inscriptions), including the visually more repellent ones, and helped me to form a life-long taste for the things.

Life had its complications for a student of the School in those days. The museums were not properly open, many hours had to be spent queuing up outside shabby offices in Athens for various permits, and contacts with the other foreign Schools were patchy. I spent much of my time either on trips to different parts of Greece to get to know the main ancient sites, or in the library developing a new topic – for the work that could be done there on Heraclitus was limited, it being primarily archaeological and therefore weak in the obscurer sources like Clement of Alexandria or Hippolytus of Rome.

This new and quite unphilosophical topic was the problem of a series of depictions of ship-scenes on Greek vases – mostly known, as indeed was the work of Heraclitus, only in fragments – of the Geometric style, current from the early ninth to the end of the eighth century B.C. It was a not unimportant matter in its way since so little was known about the history and military status of Athens in particular (where most of these vases were painted), let alone about ships, in that so-called Dark Age. Interest in the Geometric period was at its height just after the war, stimulated by German

211

excavations of the Kerameikos cemetery in Athens in the middle and late 1930s. What I did was to track down, assemble and analyze the fifty or so ship-fragments then known and discuss the likely reasons for the popularity of ship-scenes, especially in martial contexts, at this period; also the details of construction of contemporary warships, including such crucial matters as whether they were fully or only partially decked, and had one bank of oarsmen or two. Geometric style made this last matter curiously difficult to determine, since perspective was erratically applied by these primitive artists, so that a silhouette of a ship under oar would show the further file of rowers as above (and apparently sitting almost on top of) the nearer one. Moreover historians like Thucydides were themselves uncertain, two or three centuries later, of the construction of these early men-of-war, predecessors of the triremes whose shape and performance have now been so dramatically reconstructed by J. S. Morrison and J. F. Coates.

I did not finish this particular piece of work – in which a degree of practical experience of small craft in the Aegean was admittedly quite helpful here and there – until the following year, back in England, where I acquired for it by accident a most distinguished reader. On a visit to Oxford one day I inadvertently sat down in the place in the Ashmolean library reserved by custom for the almost god-like Sir John Beazley, the greatest authority by far on Greek painted pottery of a more developed kind. I happened to leave the typescript of my article on the table in front of me while I disappeared for an hour or so into the library's inner recesses in search of obscure references. When I returned, the frail old man himself was sitting there, halfway through my piece; and said with an air of charming humility 'I suppose you *meant* me to read this?' Halting apologies led to my being asked home to tea, where I met the formidable and oriental-looking Lady Beazley, under whose stern protection the great man pursued his brilliant labours. Eventually my paper was published, quite a lengthy affair of fifty pages or so, in the *Annual of the*

British School at Athens for 1947; it is still sometimes cited half a century later, which gives me special pleasure since it was my first published work, and was accomplished in such pleasant surroundings and with such delightful sponsors.

Among other episodes of that year in Greece that impressed me greatly was a trip down to Crete to stay in the Villa Ariadne at Knossos in Crete, once Sir Arthur Evans's house and now belonging to the British School at Athens. It was a rambling building surrounded by pine trees, on a low hill just above one end of the Minoan palace, over which the School in those days still ruled by almost prescriptive right. Things were very different in Knossos then: no huge car-park full of coaches, and the charm of the bare surrounding hillsides undisturbed by touristic clamour. It took many hours each day to work one's way through the ruins and find out what was what, helped by Sir Arthur's lavish seven-volume publication *The Palace of Minos* more, perhaps, than by his equally lavish concrete restorations on the site itself.

Then in the evenings an improbable bout of festivities would begin, involving on the one hand those of us staying in the villa, on the other the Greek villagers from the tiny hamlet bordering the ruins. An amiable young ex-Army officer, John Houseman, had just become engaged to Philia, the pretty daughter of the School foreman, so that Anglo-Greek relations were particularly close. Bouzoukia were played, Greek dances were danced, songs were sung (often involving, as in so much of the popular music of Europe, the dark eyes of lovely damsels), a great deal of raw Cretan wine was drunk. An eccentric, learned and extremely lovable figure, 'Squire' Hutchinson, joined in these celebrations with an enthusiasm that later earned him a stern rebuke from Athens; for he was head of this Cretan branch of the British School and should, it was thought, have brought a more sobre influence to bear. But since a highly respectable visitor from Oxford, the distinguished epigraphist Anne Jeffery – my companion on many delightful walks around the Palace of Minos and through the enchanting countryside – joined in the evening rituals with as

Some prominent members of the flotilla: Turnbull, Thwaites, Barclay, Ballantine and Fletcher.

Passage-making in Turkish waters.

214

much enjoyment as the rest of us, I can only suppose that they were in fact, as they seemed at the time, no more than entirely innocent and pleasurable evocations of what the Greeks call *kephi*, a special local version of general Mediterranean *joie de vivre.*

At all events that side of Greece and its people helped to cement (as I contemplated an imminent return to Cambridge and to sterner forms of duty) a passion for the place that has stayed with me through life; one that arose first from ancient Greek literature, and then from the adventures I have tried to record in these pages, into the heart of Homer's wine-dark Aegean itself.